tamales

tamales

FAST AND DELICIOUS MEXICAN MEALS

Alice Guadalupe Tapp

Photography by SARA REMINGTON

TEN SPEED PRESS
Berkeley

Contents

Introduction

I LOVE TAMALES. I love making them, and I love to create new varieties. I love making the masa and the fillings, and I love the process of assembling them. Most of all, I love to serve them to my family and friends and experience the satisfaction they get when tasting all the new and different flavors. They have been my ever-so-eager tamale-tasting guinea pigs for many years.

Shortly after my first book, *Tamales 101*, was published, I began teaching tamale-cooking classes at various culinary schools on the West Coast. I enjoyed teaching the process and knew the classes would increase the visibility of my book. I quickly realized that, for most students, making traditional tamales was too prep-intensive and time-consuming. Many of the students came away from those classes saying they would most likely not make the tamales at home because they were "too much work" and that they would be perfectly happy to purchase them at our tamale shop. This proved to be an excellent vehicle to promote my business; however, I truly want to keep the tamale-making tradition alive and encourage my students to make their own—I strongly believe the best tamales come from our own kitchens.

To help preserve this tradition, I began trying to come up with new methods to simplify the process and make it easier and more appealing for home cooks. It took me several years of research and trial and error, but the idea to make simple and great-tasting tamales became a mission of sorts.

My memories of cooking with my mother as a child helped me tremendously. In addition to teaching me everything she knew about tamale making, she taught me how to use time-saving techniques and products—such as ready-made moles and canned roasted chiles—to make recipes faster and easier, without compromising taste, richness, or satisfaction in the end result.

In addition to experimenting with shortening the process, which can often include up to ten steps, I experimented with different tamale styles. Tamales can be wrapped and assembled in a variety of ways, from quick and easy corundas, where the filling and masa are mixed together, to "inside-out" tamales, where the fillings are served on top or on the side of plain, unfilled tamales called *tontos*. Both of these styles can be assembled in only two or three steps. And if you can shorten the process and change up the style, who says you can't experiment with fillings, too? If you like a particular food, it will probably work in or on a tamale or corunda.

In today's world, we are so often busy and pushed for time, and the idea of setting aside one or two days to make tamales is saved for special occasions, such as Christmas, when women in Mexico traditionally gather to make traditional tamales in enormous quantities. But we should also be able to enjoy tamales on a weeknight! All of the recipes in this book shorten the process to less than an hour, once the fillings are prepared (many of which can be made well in advance), making tamales a more accessible, everyday menu item. If you would like to try your hand at tamale making but have found it to be too daunting a task, this book is especially for you.

I grew up in a kitchen, learning to cook mainly from my mother, an artist who dreamed of becoming an opera singer. Like many women of her generation, she married and had children instead. All of her artistic ability then went into cooking and homemaking. We were a culinary family, though, and my grandfather, grandmother, and aunts also helped teach me to cook.

All of my first books were cookbooks, and I still have my mother's torn, stained, falling-apart copy of *The Good Housekeeping Cookbook*. I've patched and taped it countless times over the years. I have old, brown, and stained small pieces of paper and index cards that are inscribed with recipes, mostly the favorites my grandmother, mother, and mother-in-law used. I began collecting recipes in my late teens. I asked everyone and anyone who had a good recipe to share it. For many years I would ask for the exact recipe, but eventually I was able to just get the list of ingredients and figure it out myself.

With an abundance of experience from my career in the entertainment business and establishing my own successful businesses, I wanted to create a business involving my love of tamales. My daughter, Tamara, and I opened our tamale specialty shop, Tamara's Tamales, in the Marina del Rey area of Los Angeles. We have had continued success for nineteen years. Tamara now runs the shop on a daily basis and I help with a few of the details. When asked what I attribute our success to, I usually reply that our product is good, we always put the financial well-being of the business first, and Tamara and I work well together—we love and respect each other and are grateful for our shared creative process. Also, the fact that we've always loved having our tamale business and always loved our customers doesn't hurt! Along the way, the success of Tamara's Tamales has lead to a bunch of other fun and rewarding opportunities, such as teaching tamale-making classes at culinary schools, earning top honors at tamale contests, recognition from many well-known chefs, and being able to make donations of tamales to nonprofits and benefits.

GLUTEN FREE
The recipes in this book are completely gluten free. Traditional tamales are 99.9 percent gluten free, usually containing gluten only when bread crumbs or flour are used to thicken mole sauces or roux. However, many Latin cooks use corn masa or corn tortillas for thickening sauces, which is the perfect option for those on a gluten-free diet. Be careful, though, when purchasing any type of canned, bottled, frozen, or freshly prepared moles and always check the ingredients for any added gluten in the form of thickeners, stabilizers, and so on.

Saving Time

One way to save time when making tamales is to use what you already have in your pantry, cupboard, refrigerator, or freezer. It isn't necessary to make an extra trip to the store for many items we use every day, and tamales lend themselves well to improvising. The following items are good to have on hand:

- Canned beans

- Canned chiles

- Canned chicken broth and beef broth

- Canned enchilada sauce, red and/or green

- Canned green pasilla or poblano chiles

- Canned jalapeño and serrano chiles

- Canned soups

- Canned tomatoes, tomato sauce, tomato puree, and tomato paste

- Canned tuna

- Canned vegetables

- Fresh onion, garlic, carrots, celery, and herbs

- Frozen banana leaves, precut and ready to use (these are fabulous because freezing makes them pliable, so no precooking is required to soften them)

- Frozen packages of green chiles (poblano, pasilla, New Mexico green)

- Frozen ready-to-use condiments

- Frozen tubs or packages of chile pastes

- Frozen vegetables

- Ground chicken, turkey, pork, lamb, and beef

- Packaged dried corn husks (already cleaned and ready to soak)

- Prepared bottled and fresh pestos

- Prepared cooked or stewed chicken, pork, or beef (from the deli case)

- Prepared fresh mole pastes (black, red, green, and yellow)

- Prepared fresh salsas, found in the deli case at supermarkets

- Quick Masa (page 18)

- Shredded cheese or packaged sliced cheese

The following tips will get you thinking about ways to make easy fillings:

- Use canned chopped tomatoes, tomato puree, tomato paste, and fresh tomatoes instead of tomato sauce.

- Use frozen white corn in lieu of fresh corn cut from the cob.

- Cook meats and beans in your slow cooker, following the manufacturer's directions.

- Cook meats and fillings in a pressure cooker, following the manufacturer's directions.

- Mix all of your fillings together, including raw meat, instead of cooking them separately.

- Use Quick Masa (page 18) to speed up the process.

Assembling Tamales

To assemble tamales, I recommend choosing one type of assembly method and sticking to it until you master it—you will get extremely fast, guaranteed. Then move on to trying other types. For beginners, I suggest using the corn husk fold-over type (see page 10), then wrapped in parchment; it is the easiest to master.

The problem most people have when applying the masa to the corn husk wrapper is spreading it evenly, so I have devised a simpler way that doesn't require learning the spreading technique. Alternatively, you could use a masa spreader, a relatively new tool on the market, to make spreading easier. Once you master the hand technique outlined below, though, you shouldn't have any trouble.

1   Soak the husks, if using corn husks, or use frozen banana leaves, cut into square portions.

2   Make the masa or use the masa you have prepared ahead of time.

3   Make the filling or assemble the ingredients for your corundas.

4   Assemble the tamales (see below), refrigerate them, and then steam the next day. Or assemble the tamales and freeze them raw, then cook when desired.

5   Steam tamales by placing them in a large steamer pot, which has a steaming separator with holes in it and a space for water in the bottom of the pot, under the tamales. Stack tamales loosely with the sauce-side up, the folded-side down (this prevents the sauce from running out). For bundle or other tied tamales, stack them loosely, one layer on top of the other, each layer supporting the next, to allow the steam to flow up and around them. Fill the bottom of the steamer with water to the maximum level (to prevent scorching). Bring to a fast rolling boil with high steam output, cover, and start timing according to the recipe. Reduce the heat to medium-high. Check the water level at the halfway point and add boiling hot water if needed.

CORN HUSK TAMALES: Place the scoop of masa at the wide end of the husk, wet your palm with water, and push down the masa to flatten and cover the top half of the leaf. Place your filling in the center of the masa and fold over and up, then tie with butcher string or strips of husk. Wrap the corn-husk package in parchment if desired (this is especially helpful with messier fillings). (See diagrams on pages 10 to 12 for assistance.)

BANANA LEAF TAMALES: Place the scoop of masa in the center of your banana leaf, wet your palm, and push the masa down to flatten it to about $1/4$ inch thick and wide enough to accommodate the filling placed on top,

making about a 4- to 5-inch square. Place the filling in the center, fold the sides over so the entire filling and masa are covered with each of the folds, and then tie with butcher string or strips of banana leaf to make a square package of sorts. (See diagrams on page 13 for assistance.)

Freezing Tips

You can freeze tamales at any stage.

To freeze tamales after they have been steamed (cooked), place the tamales in zip-top freezer bags and freeze indefinitely. To heat them, steam straight out of the freezer for 30 to 35 minutes over high heat.

To freeze tamales raw after they have been assembled, but before they have been cooked, stand them up in a bowl or casserole dish, keeping the open end up (so your fillings and/or masa don't spill or ooze out). Freeze the tamales and then, when the tamales are frozen, place them in zip-top freezer bags and return the bags to the freezer.

To freeze prepared masa dough, place portions in zip-top freezer bags. Completely flatten the masa in the bag and squeeze to remove all the air.

To freeze the unprepared masa, simply freeze the package of wet masa you bring home from the supermarket. You can also freeze the fillings and sauces separately, before assembling the tamales; they can then be defrosted and assembled anytime.

CORUNDAS

Corundas are the style of tamale in which the ingredients are all mixed into the masa itself. Savory or sweet, they are simple to create and assemble—just mix the masa and filling together, then wrap and steam as you would a regular tamale. See recipes on pages 66, 107 to 109, and 122 to 127 for more information.

ALL SCOOPS ARE NOT CREATED EQUAL

Most of us already have scoops in our kitchens. For tamales, I use the type with the spring-loaded release lever. These are the best type to use, rather than an ice cream scoop, where you need to slide the ingredients off the scoop with your finger. If you already have the lever type, you'll just want to measure the amount it holds. You can do this by filling it up with water and then pouring the water into a measuring cup. If it's smaller or larger than what each recipe calls for, just remember your tamale yield will be different. It's great to have two scoops, one for the masa and one for the filling; however, if you have only one, you can apply the masa on the leaves all at one time, and then clean the scoop and use it to place the filling on the masa in each tamale.

Corn Husk Wrapping Styles

TIED AT BOTH ENDS

1. Spread the masa across the center, at least 1 inch from the flat end of the husk.

2. Fold both sides in tightly to overlap.

3. Twist one end of the husk and tie, then twist the other end and tie.

FOLD-OVER METHOD

1. Spread the masa across the center, $1/4$ inch from the flat end of the husk.

2. Fold both sides in tightly to overlap.

3. Fold the pointed end up to meet the flat end.

FOLD-OVER WITH ONE TIE

1. Spread the masa across the center, $1/4$ inch from the flat end of the husk.

2. Fold both sides in tightly to overlap.

3. Fold the pointed end up to meet the flat end.

4. Tie around the middle.

FOLD-OVER WITH TWO TIES

1. Spread the masa across the center, 1/4 inch from the flat end of the husk.

2. Fold both sides in tightly to overlap.

3. Fold up the pointed end toward the center of the husk.

4. Tie once, 1 inch from the top and once, 1 inch from the bottom.

CORUNDA-STYLE

1. Place the masa scoop in the center of the husk, 1 inch from the flat end of the husk.

2. Fold both sides in tightly to overlap.

3. Fold the pointed end up to meet the flat end.

4. Twist the ends of the husk together and tie at the top.

CORUNDA-STYLE WITH A TIE AROUND THE MIDDLE

1. Spread the masa across the center, 1 inch from the flat end of the husk.

2. Fold both sides in tightly to overlap, then fold up the pointed end toward the center of the husk.

3. Tie once around the middle, securing the folded-over, pointed end; then twist the flat end and tie at the top.

CORUNDA-STYLE USING TWO HUSKS

1. Place the masa scoop at the flat end of one husk.

2. Fold both sides in tightly to overlap.

3. Wrap the flat end of a second husk around the first.

4. Fold up the pointed end of the second husk toward the center of the husks.

5. Secure the second husk's pointed end with one tie, then twist the first husk's pointed end and tie at the top.

SMALL SQUARE PACKAGE

1. Spread the masa into a small square shape in the center of the husk.

2. Fold both sides in tightly to overlap, then fold the pointed and flat ends in tightly to overlap.

3. Tie horizontally and vertically, then finish with a knot or bow.

BANANA LEAF WRAPPING STYLES

SQUARE PACKAGE

1. Spread the masa into a square shape in the center of the leaf.

2. Fold both sides in tightly to overlap, then fold the top and bottom ends tightly to overlap.

3. Tie horizontally and/or vertically, then finish with a knot or bow.

RECTANGULAR PACKAGE

 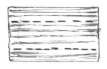  

1. Spread the masa into a rectangular shape in the center of the leaf.

2. Fold the top and bottom ends in tightly to overlap.

3. Fold the sides in toward the center of the leaf.

4. Tie to secure both folded-over sides.

Masa

LET'S TALK MASA. Masa is the plain, wet, stone-ground corn dough made with a special corn known as nixtamal. It's sold two different ways—prepared and unprepared. Prepared masa is plain masa that has been mixed with lard and salt only. This type of masa yields a heavy, greasy, drier dough. For many of the recipes in this book, use unprepared masa and prepare it as directed for a perfectly light and flavorful dough. Because it's one of the most important ingredients, correctly preparing the masa is essential.

TYPES OF MASA

This chapter features a few types of masa, all of which work well and are corn based. The variety of masa recipes allows you to pick your favorites and experiment with different types depending on your taste and the ingredients available. The types of masa that I consistently use for making tamales are traditional stone-ground fresh masa and cooked masa harina.

TRADITIONAL STONE-GROUND FRESH MASA: This type is made from nixtamal, dried white dent corn. The kernels are boiled for approximately 20 minutes in a water and slaked lime solution. The corn then steeps for 12 to 24 hours to loosen the hard outer shell, called the pericarp, and hydrate the starch in the center of the kernel. The corn is then put through a washing, rinsing, and rubbing process to remove the loosened pericarp and the excess lime solution. The washed kernels are finally ground with a stone grinder to form the masa used to make tortillas and tamales.

PREPARED STONE-GROUND FRESH MASA: This is made from nixtamal and sold with the lard and salt already added.

DRIED MASA HARINA: Dried white dent corn kernels are ground into a fine flour. This is corn flour, not to be confused with cornmeal.

COOKED MASA HARINA: This is a dough made with dried corn flour, broth, butter or lard, and salt.

Quick Masa

To be able to make tamales any time, prepare a batch of masa and freeze it in gallon-size plastic bags. You can usually buy your masa in 5-pound bags or wrapped portions. Divide the 5 pounds in half and make two batches of prepared masa; each batch will yield two gallon-size bags of prepared masa for a total of four bags. Two and a half pounds of fresh (wet) unprepared masa fits perfectly into the bowl of a stand mixer; you can make the whole 5 pounds at once, but it takes longer and just barely fits in the bowl.

MAKES 2 GALLON-SIZE BAGS, EACH BAG YIELDS 24 (¼-CUP SCOOP) TAMALES

2½ pounds stone ground fresh masa (unprepared)

¾ cup stock (chicken, beef, pork, or vegetable)

2 tablespoons butter, margarine, or lard

1½ teaspoons salt

Combine all the ingredients in the bowl of a stand mixer and on low speed to start, then mix on high speed. Pinch off a small piece of dough and place in a small cup of cold water. If it floats to the top, the dough is ready. If not, continue mixing and test again.

Divide the dough in half and place each in a gallon-size zip-top freezer bag. Completely flatten the masa in the bag and squeeze to remove all the air. Freeze until ready to use.

To defrost the prepared masa, lay the bag in the direct sunlight or in a warm place, or run under warm water.

Cooked Masa Harina

You'll love the results you get making this type of masa, which has a fantastic texture and taste. Masa harina is available at most supermarkets and is usually what is used in South American cooking. Many cooks flavor their masa with chili powder, chile sauce, and/or minced onion and garlic.

MAKES 12 TO 24 TAMALES, DEPENDING ON SIZE

6 cups masa harina (dried corn flour)

4 cups stock (chicken, pork, beef, or vegetable)

2 cups lard, butter, or margarine, melted

2 teaspoons salt

In a large bowl, combine, by hand, the corn flour and stock. Add the melted fat and salt and mix again. This can be done with a mixer, but it comes together so easily and doesn't require the extra beating to fluff it. Place the mixture in a pot large enough to hold all of it. Bring it to a boil over medium heat, stirring constantly.

Continue to stir for 30 minutes, until the masa is cooked. If you've ever made polenta, it's the same idea. The flour absorbs the liquid, expands, and becomes dense but fluffy during the cooking process.

Masa Harina Tamale Masa

Many good tamales are made with dry corn flour, known as masa harina (flour) or masa seca (dry). Easily found in large chain grocery stores, it is convenient and actually the preferred masa used by many cooks and *tamaleras*. You may also add garlic powder and chili powder to punch up the taste. MAKES 24 TO 36 TAMALES

12 cups masa harina (dried corn flour)

10 to 12 cups warm stock (chicken, pork, beef, or vegetable)

3 cups lard, shortening, butter, or margarine, melted

2 tablespoons salt

For this amount of masa, you'll need a very large bowl. Measure all the corn flour into the bowl. Add the warm stock, melted lard, and salt. Mix well until the texture is a soft, thick paste, adding additional stock if needed to achieve consistency. Continue mixing by hand, use a hand mixer, or place in a stand mixer and whip at high speed until a small piece of dough floats when placed in a cup of cold water. Set aside until ready to use.

Basic Fresh Masa

To make this type of masa dough, my grandmother used lard, and my mother used vegetable shortening or a combination of both. I switched to butter. Traditional cooks use even more fat than what is called for here, but I think this 1:5 ratio of butter to masa is perfect. Feel free to use your preference of lard, shortening, butter, or margarine.

MAKES ABOUT 60 TAMALES

1 pound butter or margarine, softened

5 pounds stone ground fresh masa (unprepared)

2 to 3 cups stock (chicken, pork, beef, or vegetable)

2 tablespoons salt (or less to taste)

Place the butter in the bowl of a stand mixer and whip until fluffy, about 2 minutes. Add one-third of the fresh masa alternating with one-third of the stock, then add the salt. Beat until well mixed, adding more stock if needed, turn the mixer to high, and beat for 3 to 5 minutes, or until the dough resembles spackling paste.

Take a small piece (about $1/2$ teaspoon) of the dough and drop it into a cup of cold water. If it floats, it is ready; if it sinks, whip for another minute and test it again. Repeat this process until the masa floats.

Note: The fresher the masa, the faster it will become light and fluffy enough for use.

Polenta Masa

Several years ago, a customer came into the shop and told me she was moving to Italy and was going to miss our tamales. Off the top of my head, I told her she could make them herself using polenta for the masa and fresh cornhusks to wrap them. She was delighted! I have since tried it to great results. Here is my answer to making masa anywhere in the world.

MAKES ABOUT 12 TAMALES

4 cups water, or 2 cups milk and 2 cups water

1 cup cornmeal (I use Albers or Bob's Red Mill Corn Grits)

3 to 4 tablespoons butter

1/2 teaspoon salt

In a medium saucepan, bring the water and milk to a boil over high heat. Slowly add the cornmeal, while beating with a whisk. Cover, reduce the heat to medium-low, and cook for approximately 7 minutes, stirring occasionally to prevent sticking.

Add the butter and salt and continue to whisk for another 5 minutes. Pour into a buttered 8-inch square pan and allow to cool. Cut into squares.

To assemble your tamales, use one square for each tamale, placing it onto your corn husk. With the palm of your hand, flatten the polenta onto the husk, fill your tamale, and wrap.

Note: Grits can be used as an alternative to cornmeal.

Store-Bought Prepared Masa

Masa preparada (prepared masa) has already had fat added to it, though probably more than you would add yourself. It's available at Latin markets and is extremely easy to make—all you need to do is add the stock and mix it in a mixer to fluff it up. Do not use it right out of the package because it will be too dry to use without the stock. Many excellent Mexican cooks use it, so I'm including it here for your convenience. It would be a good idea to taste it first, because salt is usually already added.

MAKES ABOUT 60 TAMALES

5 pounds *masa preparada* (prepared masa)

2 to 3 cups stock (chicken or whatever you prefer)

Salt, as needed

Place the masa in the bowl of a stand mixer, or use a bowl and handheld mixer, add half the stock, and mix gently on low speed until combined. Add $1/2$ cup stock, mixing on low for 20 to 30 seconds to combine.

Continue whipping the masa on medium-high, adding more stock as needed, until a small piece floats to the top of a cup water. Taste for salt and add if needed.

Vegan Masa

This masa is for those who follow plant-based diets or just prefer using olive oil to lard or butter. You may also use this masa to make vegan pupusas and tortillas. The results have the same texture and excellent taste. MAKES 30 TO 60 TAMALES, DEPENDING ON SIZE

1 cup margarine or vegetable shortening, chilled, or olive oil

2^1/$_2$ pounds stone ground fresh masa (unprepared)

2 cups vegetable stock

1^1/$_2$ teaspoons salt

2 to 4 tablespoons dried mushroom powder, store-bought or homemade (see Note)

If you use the margarine or shortening, place it in a mixing bowl and whip for 2 to 3 minutes, until light and fluffy. Add the masa and beat for 1 minute more, then add the stock, a little at a time, then add the salt and mushroom powder to taste. Continue beating for 2 to 4 minutes, or until a pinch of masa floats to the top of a cup of water.

If using the olive oil, pour it into shallow casserole dish, cover, and place in the freezer for at least 24 hours. Remove right before using. It should be frozen to the hard stage. The temperature and the dense, solidified consistency help the masa remain light and fluffy during cooking. Combine the frozen oil and the masa in a mixing bowl and beat together for 1 to 2 minutes. Add the stock a little at a time, then add the salt and mushroom powder and beat until light and fluffy, 4 to 5 minutes, or until a pinch of dough floats to the top of a cup of water.

Note: Making homemade mushroom powder is simple. Place any type of dried mushrooms in a food processor and process into a fine powder.

Sweet Masa

For most dessert tamale recipes, you will need to use this very easy-to-make masa. It is also easy to halve, double, or triple this recipe.

MAKES 6 TO 12 TAMALES

3 cups masa of your choice, prepared

¹/₄ cup sugar or brown sugar

1 tablespoon vanilla extract

Combine all the ingredients in a medium-size bowl and mix together by hand until completely integrated.

Sauces and Salsas

SAUCES AND SALSAS ARE QUITE EASY TO MAKE, especially if you used simplified versions of more traditional recipes, such as the recipes in this chapter. Once you've mastered the basic sauce components—chiles, tomatoes, onion, garlic, herbs, salt, sometimes sugar, and acid (lemon juice, lime juice, or vinegar)—you can even start improvising your own sauces.

HOW TO BUILD A SALSA

It's so easy to build a sauce, and you can use what you have on hand, such as the following:

- Tomato sauce—15-ounce can or 28-ounce can

- Chiles—either 1 fresh minced jalapeño or a 7-ounce can of chopped chiles, or both

- Onion—chopped white or green onion

- Garlic—1 teaspoon powdered garlic

- Herbs—1 teaspoon dried oregano, 1 teaspoon cumin powder

- Salt and pepper

- Optional—a squeeze of lemon or lime juice (fresh, frozen, or bottled) or 1 tablespoon any type of vinegar (apple cider, white, regular or white balsamic, or rice)

Now let's use that salsa to make a sauce. Heat $^1/_4$ cup oil in a skillet or saucepan, add the salsa, and gently cook over low to medium-low heat for about 25 minutes. Now you have a tomato-based chile sauce.

Sauces using dried chile pods are just as easy—see Super Easy Chile Paste (page 34) and Super Easy Red Chile Pasilla Sauce (page 36). Or build your own using the chile pods as your base ingredient and adding the other components to it (listed above) as your guide.

HOW TO BUILD A SAUCE

1   Start with your base. Usually this will be chunkier and vegetable based, such as fresh or canned tomatoes.

2   Add heat. Choose your favorite red or green chiles or use what you have on hand—fresh, dried, canned, bottled, powdered, granulated, or frozen all work. Finely mince and add to the base.

3   Add onion. Brown, white, red, or green onions work, and even chives or leeks can be used. Fresh, chopped and packaged, flaked, powdered, or frozen are all suitable.

4   Add garlic. Fresh, whole cloves already peeled and packaged, packed in olive oil, crushed frozen, jarred minced, dried ground, garlic powder, or garlic flakes all work. Mince fresh garlic finely.

5   Finish with herbs—fresh, dried, or frozen. Oregano, cilantro, cumin, mint, and chives are all good options.

Super Easy Avocado Sauce

If you want more heat in this sauce, add your favorite green chiles (fresh, canned, or bottled). This is great served over a tonto; as a dip for chips; as a dressing for salads; and as a sauce for tacos, enchiladas, chilaquiles, quesadillas, burritos, or plain tortillas. For a creamier variation, mix in 1 to 2 tablespoons of cream, sour cream, or half-and-half, taste, and add salt if needed. MAKES 2³/₄ CUPS

2 cups Super Easy
Tomatillo Salsa (page 39)

1 large avocado

Good pinch of salt

Good pinch of pepper

Place all the ingredients in a food processor or blender and process for 10 to 15 seconds, until smooth. Use immediately or store in the refrigerator until ready to use, a couple of hours at the most.

SUPER EASY
CHILE VERDE SAUCE
(PAGE 35)

SUPER EASY
CHILE PASTE
(PAGE 34)

SUPER EASY RED
PASILLA CHILE SAUCE
(PAGE 36)

SUPER EASY
TOMATILLO SALSA
(PAGE 39)

SUPER EASY
AVOCADO SAUCE
(OPPOSITE)

SUPER EASY SALSA
(PAGE 37)

Super Easy Chile Paste

This is the basic recipe for any type of chile paste, to which you can add tomato sauce, chicken broth, and a small amount of salt. It is simple and can be used for enchiladas, chilaquiles, soups, meats, stews, tacos, and of course, tamales. MAKES ³/₄ TO 1 CUP PASTE

6 to 8 dried pasilla, ancho, California, negro, or guajillo chiles, or a combination

1 teaspoon ground cumin

1 teaspoon oregano

2 teaspoons sugar

Remove the stems and seeds from the dried chiles. Place in a medium bowl and cover with boiling water. Place a plate over the bowl and allow to steep for 20 to 30 minutes, until the chiles are soft.

Place the chiles in a food processor or blender and process until a smooth paste is formed, adding a small amount of the soaking liquid, if needed. Add the remaining ingredients and process until smooth. The paste can be refrigerated for up to a few days or frozen for later use.

Super Easy Chile Verde Sauce

This sauce is so simple you'll use it over and again for all your green chile recipes. It's especially good with pork, chicken, or cheese tamales. You can double the recipe and freeze it in jars or plastic containers (2- or 4-cup portions) to have it on hand. MAKES 4 CUPS

3 tablespoons olive oil

1 (28-ounce) can green chile enchilada sauce (I use Las Palmas)

2 (7-ounce) cans whole or chopped Ortega chiles

2 teaspoons onion powder

2 teaspoons sugar

1/4 to 1/2 teaspoon salt

Heat the olive oil in a medium saucepan. Add all of the ingredients and bring to a medium boil. Simmer for 15 minutes, checking and stirring often. Set aside to cool or refrigerate until ready to use. This can also be frozen.

Super Easy Red Pasilla Chile Sauce

A simple version of the famous red chile sauce, this recipe cuts the preparation time down from 2 hours or more to 45 minutes. If you have leftover sauce, make enchiladas or chilaquiles. If the sauce is too hot, add 16 ounces of tomato sauce. If you want more heat, use New Mexico hot dried chiles instead of the pasilla chiles, which are milder. MAKES 7 CUPS

1 (2-ounce) package dried pasilla chiles, stemmed and seeded, or 4 tablespoons prepared chile paste

2 (28-ounce) cans enchilada sauce

1 teaspoon oregano

2 teaspoons sugar

$1/2$ teaspoon cumin

$1/2$ teaspoon salt

$1/4$ teaspoon pepper

$1/4$ cup olive oil

Place the cleaned chiles in a medium bowl and pour boiling water to cover, place a dish on top to keep the heat in, and set aside for 20 to 30 minutes, until the chiles are completely soft. Place the chiles into a food processor or blender and process until you have a smooth paste, then add the enchilada sauce, oregano, sugar, cumin, salt, and pepper and process or blend until well combined, about 5 to 10 seconds.

Heat the olive oil in a large pan and add the sauce, cover, and cook over medium heat for 15 minutes, checking and stirring occasionally to make sure the sauce doesn't burn. Set aside to cool. The sauce can be refrigerated or frozen for future use.

Super Easy Salsa

I have used this recipe for many years. I got it at a restaurant in Southern California and have used it ever since; it is super simple and really good.

MAKES 2 CUPS

1 (11.5-ounce) can V8 juice, chilled

¹/₂ minced fresh jalapeño, seeded if desired

¹/₄ cup minced or chopped cilantro

¹/₄ teaspoon oregano

1 teaspoon fresh lime or lemon juice or vinegar

Salt, as needed

Mix everything together and taste, adding salt a pinch at a time if needed. Serve with chips or use as a sauce. Refrigerate between uses.

Super Easy Tomatillo Salsa

This sauce uses canned tomatillos in place of fresh or freshly cooked ones, which are traditionally used. It can be used to sauce meat, chicken, or fish, or for casseroles and enchiladas. The sweetener is needed to cut the acidity of the canned tomatillos. MAKES ABOUT 2$^1/_2$ CUPS

1 (28-ounce) can tomatillos

1 large clove garlic, or $^1/_2$ teaspoon crushed garlic

$^1/_2$ to 1 fresh jalapeño

1 small, $^1/_2$ medium, or $^1/_4$ large onion

$^1/_2$ bunch fresh cilantro leaves

$^1/_4$ teaspoon salt, or less to taste

$^1/_2$ teaspoon sugar

Place all the ingredients in a food processor or blender and pulse until you have a heavy salsa with small chunks. Use immediately or refrigerate or freeze for future use.

Inside-Out Tamales

I CALL THESE TAMALES "INSIDE OUTS," because the fillings are not inside the tamale but are served on top. The tamales used in these recipes are called tontos, which means "dummies" in Spanish. The tontos are made entirely of masa dough and are fast and easy to prepare. If you like corn tortillas, you will love tontos.

Growing up, we always made tontos if there was leftover masa at the end of our tamale-making sessions. We ate them warm with butter and sour cream drizzled over the top; floating in chicken, albóndiga (meatballs), or other types of soup; or as an accompaniment to a good bowl of beans, with or without toppings of cheese, sour cream, onion, and cilantro.

The fillings, or "inside outs," can be as diverse as that in any regular tamale, and in many cases more so. Sometimes, what should make a delicious tamale filling just doesn't quite work because steaming makes it too tough or too mushy. Tamales are made with fillings that are usually already cooked. Then when they are steamed, it essentially cooks the filling for a second time while the masa around it cooks, binding to the filling, which flavors the masa. Shrimp, for example, will become rubbery inside a regular tamale after the steaming process. But shrimp is too good not to have with a tamale, so I eventually figured out a solution, using it as a topping on an inside-out tamale.

Having a supply of the plain tontos in the freezer and serving them with your favorite filling—or topping, shall we say—is a very simple way to still have the tamale experience, with a lot less work involved.

Tontos

Because tontos are all masa, you'll want to make them a little larger, so use at least $^1/_2$ cup for each one. They can be made with any type of masa you wish to use. I love tontos with as simple a topping as melted butter, a good dollop of sour cream, and a little bit of salt. MAKES 12 TONTOS

6 cups Basic Fresh Masa (page 21) or Cooked Masa Harina (page 19)

12 large corn husks or banana leaves

Using $^1/_2$ cup masa per tamale, scoop the masa onto the husk or leaves, wrap, and steam for 45 to 50 minutes.

Cactus and Bean Inside-Out Tamales

This recipe for beans and nopales (cactus) was given to me by my aunt Renie, who always made it for special occasions. To make an easier version, you can use a 30-ounce jar of sliced cactus (nopalitos), rinsed, and a 14-ounce can of whole tomatoes (including the liquid) instead of fresh tomatoes. If you aren't familiar with nopales, they have a mild, leafy flavor similar to that of lettuce. They tend to have a slightly slimy texture—not as much as okra, but similar. Rinsing them several times in water will help minimize it. SERVES 8 TO 10

1 pound fresh cactus, sliced, spines removed

1/2 pound thick-cut bacon, thinly sliced

1 medium onion, chopped

4 large cloves garlic, minced

1 pound fresh tomatoes, chopped

2 fresh serrano chiles, seeded and minced

2 to 3 cups cooked pinto beans

3 tablespoons minced cilantro

1 tablespoon minced epazote (optional)

1/8 teaspoon seasoned salt

1 teaspoon pepper

Pinch of cumin (optional)

Pinch of oregano (optional)

16 to 20 tontos (page 42)

Place the cactus in a saucepan of water and gently boil over medium-high heat for 40 minutes, or until tender. Rinse, drain, and set aside.

Slice the bacon into 1/2-inch pieces and fry in a skillet over medium heat until the fat is rendered but the bacon is not crispy. Take the bacon out of the skillet and set aside.

Sauté the onion and garlic in the bacon fat until soft, 5 to 7 minutes. Add the tomatoes and cook until the tomatoes are soft, about 20 minutes. Add the chiles and cook for 10 minutes, stirring to mix. Add the cactus, beans, bacon, cilantro, epazote, seasoned salt, pepper, cumin, and oregano. Mix well, cover, reduce the heat to medium-low, and cook for 10 to 15 minutes to blend the flavors. Taste and adjust the seasonings to taste.

Warm the tontos, place on a plate, and pour the sauce over.

Corn Salad Inside-Out Tamales

To make this easier, buy prepared corn salsa from your favorite restaurant, deli, or supermarket. If time isn't an issue, this is the best recipe for corn salad ever and is especially good when corn is in season. SERVES 4 OR 5

3 or 4 ears fresh corn

Butter, softened, as needed

$1/4$ teaspoon seasoned salt or to taste

$1/4$ teaspoon pepper or to taste

$1/3$ cup minced red or green onion

1 fresh jalapeño, stemmed, seeded if desired, and minced

$1/2$ bunch fresh cilantro

2 medium tomatoes, chopped

2 tablespoons freshly squeezed lemon juice

$1/4$ cup white balsamic or apple cider vinegar

$1/2$ cup olive oil

8 to 10 tontos (page 42)

To prepare the corn for grilling, fold back the husks but do not remove. Remove the corn silk and brush the ears with butter and sprinkle with salt and pepper. Pull the husks over the ears to cover and place on a hot grill. Grill the ears, turning frequently and burning the outer leaves, until the kernels begin to char, 15 to 20 minutes. Set aside and allow to cool.

Cut the corn from the cobs and place in a 2- or 3-quart bowl, then add the onion, jalapeño, cilantro, tomatoes, lemon juice, vinegar, and oil. Toss together and taste. Adjust the seasonings as desired. Place in the refrigerator for 1 hour or leave on the counter until ready to serve.

To serve, place 2 tontos on each of 4 or 5 plates and spoon plenty of salad over each.

Mexican Tuna Inside-Out Tamales

Many years ago, my employee Maria, who is from Jalisco, Mexico, made this tuna recipe for me, and I have used it countless times for friends and family. It is so good as presented here, and I also use it as a dip with chips or for tostadas without beans. SERVES 4

1 (6-ounce) can white albacore tuna packed in water, with liquid

$^1/_2$ cup cilantro, chopped

1 large tomato, chopped

2 tablespoons minced red or other onion

$^1/_4$ cup Mexican crema or sour cream

$^1/_4$ cup mayonnaise

2 tablespoons minced pickled jalapeño, plus 2 tablespoons juice from the jar or can

Good pinch of salt

Good pinch of black pepper

8 tontos (page 42)

In a medium-size bowl, combine the tuna, cilantro, tomato, onion, crema, mayonnaise, jalapeño and juice, and salt and pepper.

Warm the tontos, place on a platter, and spoon the tuna over. Serve.

Ratatouille Inside-Out Tamales

This recipe comes from a beloved friend, Ariana Caitlin, and is the best ratatouille I have ever tasted. I think it makes a really nice statement dish and is easy to prepare. Of course, it can be made and served as a vegetable side dish for any occasion and gets better as leftovers. It can also be made in a slow cooker. SERVES 10 TO 12

¹/₂ cup olive oil, or more as needed

1 large onion, minced

1 head garlic, peeled and left in whole cloves

1 large eggplant, chopped into 1-inch cubes

1 bell pepper, cored, seeded, and cut into 1-inch cubes

3 zucchini, sliced or cut into 1-inch cubes

2 tomatoes, chopped

¹/₂ (6-ounce) can tomato paste

6 tablespoons water

2 teaspoons finely minced lemon peel

2 teaspoons salt, or more to taste

2 teaspoons pepper, or more to taste

20 to 24 tontos (page 42)

Preheat the oven to 450°F. Add the olive oil to a large round casserole (4 quart or larger) and place in the oven. When the oil is hot, add the onion and garlic, cover, and allow to cook for a few minutes until the onion is translucent.

Mix in the eggplant, return to the oven, and let roast until the oil is soaked up, approximately 5 minutes, checking frequently. Add the bell pepper, return to the oven, and roast a few more minutes. Add the zucchini and more oil, if needed, return to the oven, and roast for a few minutes. Add the tomatoes, tomato paste, water, lemon rind, and salt and pepper and stir to combine. Lower the oven temperature to 350°F, cover, and cook until done (the eggplant will be soft and completely cooked throughout, leaving no trace of white colored flesh), 45 to 60 minutes, checking and stirring often.

Warm the tontos, place on a platter, and spoon the ratatouille over. Serve.

Delicious Shrimp Inside-Out Tamales

If you use cleaned and butterflied frozen shrimp, your prep time is cut in half. And if you have tontos in the freezer ready to use, these can be put together very quickly and easily. I have been making this recipe for pasta for many years. The slightly cooked shrimp makes all the difference in how delicious the sauce turns out. I would use this only as an inside-out variety.
SERVES 4 TO 6

3 green onions, minced

4 cloves garlic, minced

1/2 cup fresh basil leaves

1/4 cup olive oil

3 medium tomatoes, chopped

Salt and pepper

1 pound fresh large shrimp, shelled, deveined, and butterflied

8 to 12 tontos (page 42)

In a large skillet over medium heat, sauté the green onions, garlic, and basil in olive oil until soft, 3 to 4 minutes. Add the tomatoes and cook gently until a sauce begins to form, about 7 minutes, stirring often. Add salt and pepper to taste. Add the shrimp, turn the heat to medium-high, and cook for 2 minutes tops on each side, or until just translucent. Do not overcook the shrimp.

Warm the tontos, place on a platter, and spoon the shrimp mixture over; serve immediately.

Meat Tamales

OVER THE YEARS, I have made some variation of all the tamales fillings in this chapter as basic meat dishes. In addition to filling tamales with traditional sauce and meat preparations, you can adapt staple meat dish recipes as fillings. Chorizo is a basic, staple ingredient in Mexican cooking, usually added to eggs or potatoes—I have added it to other types of ground meats or beans as to spice up fillings and incorporate a ready-made, which helps make preparation easier and faster.

You can use any basic stew, casserole, bean, or soup recipe as a tamale filling. They can be made the same way you have made them for years, or you can add some type of fresh or canned chiles of your choice and/or a bit of freshly chopped cilantro for a little more Latin flair.

Chicken and Chorizo Tamales

Mexican-style chorizo is quite different than other types of chorizo, such as Spanish chorizo, which is more like sausage that can be sliced. Mexican chorizo is raw and should be sautéed before combining with other ingredients. It cannot be sliced, because it separates into small clumps when cooked. It has amazing flavor and can be used in all sorts of interesting ways—I suggest you start using it more frequently!

MAKES 12 TO 18 TAMALES

1¹/₂ pounds ground chicken

3 tablespoons olive oil

¹/₂ cup chopped onion

1 tomato, chopped

3 cloves garlic, minced

1 pound pork or beef chorizo

¹/₄ teaspoon ground cumin

¹/₄ teaspoon oregano

¹/₄ teaspoon ground thyme

¹/₄ teaspoon freshly ground pepper

1 bunch cilantro, finely chopped

3 to 4¹/₂ cups Basic Fresh Masa (page 21)

In a skillet over medium heat, lightly brown the chicken in the olive oil for 15 minutes. Add the onion, tomato, and garlic and cook for 2 to 3 minutes. Add the raw chorizo, cumin, oregano, thyme, and pepper, stir to combine, and cook for an additional 15 minutes, mixing and incorporating the chorizo as it cooks. Add the cilantro and cook for a final 2 to 3 minutes. Place in a bowl and allow to cool.

Assemble the tamales (see pages 5-6), using ¹/₄ cup masa and ¹/₄ cup filling for each tamale. Transfer to a steamer and steam for 55 minutes.

Chicken Curry Tamales

This curry base is also good when made with shrimp, lamb, or vegetables (carrots, potatoes, green beans, and chickpeas are good ones to try). And an easier version can be made with a 13-ounce jar of prepared curry sauce. Just follow the instructions on the label. This is the chicken version of our vegan-style Veggie Curry tamale, which has been a favorite of my customers for many years. MAKES 24 TAMALES

1 small onion, minced

1 large clove garlic, minced

$1/4$ cup tomato sauce, or 1 small tomato, chopped

$1/4$ cup olive oil

2 pounds uncooked chicken breast, cut into small cubes

1 cup diced potato

1 cup diced carrot

2 tablespoons curry powder

1 tablespoon chili powder

1 (14-ounce) can coconut milk, or more if needed

$4^{1}/2$ to 6 cups Basic Fresh Masa (page 21)

In a skillet over medium heat, sauté the onion, garlic, and fresh tomato (if using) in the olive oil for 4 to 5 minutes. Add the chicken, potato, and carrot and stir to combine. Cover the skillet and cook for 5 minutes. Add the curry, chili powder, coconut milk, and tomato sauce (if using) and simmer gently, stirring frequently, until the chicken and the vegetables are tender, about 15 minutes. Add more coconut milk if needed to create plenty of sauce for your tamales.

Assemble the tamales (see pages 5-6), using $1/4$ cup masa, $1/4$ cup filling, and 1 to 2 tablespoons of sauce for each tamale. Transfer to a steamer and steam for 50 minutes.

Chicken Mole Poblano Tamales

This is an easy, delicious version of chicken with Oaxacan mole sauce. The peanut butter punches it up a bit, a trick my mother taught me. She used canned, powdered mole poblano that called only for chicken broth to be added, which is what I do, too. I use Doña Maria mole poblano, a paste product that comes in small glass jars. MAKES 18 TAMALES

1 (8.5-ounce) jar prepared mole or mole poblano

2 tablespoons peanut butter

3 cups chicken stock, or 3 cups water mixed with 3 tablespoons good granulated chicken bouillon

3 cups cubed chicken

4¹/₂ cups Basic Fresh Masa (page 21)

Open the jar of mole and pour the thin layer of oil off the top of the paste into a medium saucepan. Heat the oil over medium heat and add the peanut butter. Fry the peanut butter for a couple of minutes, stirring frequently so it doesn't burn. Add the contents of the jar (you'll need a knife or fork to remove it, because it is quite dry and solid). Immediately add the chicken stock and, using a whisk, break down all the mole lumps. Simmer for 10 to 15 minutes, whisking frequently, until a very smooth sauce forms. Pour into a medium bowl and set aside to cool.

When the sauce is cool, add the chicken and stir until the chicken is well distributed into the sauce.

Assemble the tamales (see pages 5-6), using ¹/₄ cup masa and ¹/₄ cup chicken mole filling per tamale. Transfer to a steamer and steam for 55 minutes.

Note: If you are gluten free, check any prepared mole sauce for thickening agents and use only those made with corn, banana, or rice.

Chicken Sinaloa Tamales

This is a great version of Sinaloa-style tamales. Sinaloa is a state in Mexico where my father was born—Mazatlán, Puerto Vallarta, and Acapulco are all in located in Sinaloa. These tamales are simple to make with the Super Easy Red Pasilla Chile Sauce. We offer these tamales in our shop at Christmas, as it is a traditional Christmas tamale in my father's birthplace and a family favorite. MAKES 18 TAMALES

$1/4$ cup olive oil

1 small to medium onion, diced

1 medium potato, diced

1 carrot, diced

1 zucchini, diced

2 pickled jalapeños, minced

1 teaspoon salt, or to taste

1 medium tomato, diced

$1/2$ cup raisins

$1/2$ cup finely chopped green olives

3 or more cups Super Easy Red Pasilla Chile Sauce (page 36)

2 cups cubed cooked chicken

$3^1/2$ cups Basic Fresh Masa (page 21)

Heat the oil in large pot over medium heat, add the onion, and sauté for 2 to 3 minutes. Add the potato, carrot, zucchini, jalapeños, and salt and stir to combine. Sauté for 15 minutes or until the potato and carrot are barely soft. Remove from the heat and let cool. Add the tomato, raisins, olives, chile pasilla sauce, and chicken. Fold well. Taste and adjust the salt.

Assemble the tamales (see pages 5-6), using $1/4$ cup masa and $1/4$ cup filling for each tamale. Transfer to a steamer and steam for 50 minutes.

Chicken Suisa Tamales

This is an easy recipe and can be made even easier by using canned green pasilla chiles and canned tomatillos. They taste excellent with this lighter sauce and the cheeses. The word *Suisa* means "Swiss," the type of cheese used. It also refers in general to light-colored sauces made with cheese.

MAKES 24 TAMALES

1 pound ground chicken

1 small onion, chopped

2 large cloves garlic, minced

1/4 cup olive oil

1/2 teaspoon seasoned salt

1/4 teaspoon freshly ground pepper

6 large tomatillos, husked, washed, and chopped

Leaves from 1/2 bunch fresh cilantro

1 tablespoon honey or sugar

2 cups chicken stock

2 large fresh pasilla chiles, roasted, seeded, deveined, and coarsely chopped

4 1/2 to 6 cups Basic Fresh Masa (page 21)

1 cup crème fraîche or Mexican crema

1 cup grated Swiss cheese

1 cup grated Jack cheese

In a skillet over medium heat, sauté the ground chicken, onion, and garlic in the olive oil until the chicken is browned and the onion is translucent, about 20 minutes, stirring occasionally to cook evenly. Add the seasoned salt and pepper; taste and adjust the seasonings.

Meanwhile, place the tomatillos, cilantro, honey, and chicken stock in a blender and pulse into a chunky, thick sauce. Add to the cooked chicken mixture and cook for 20 minutes, or until all the flavors are well blended. Add the chiles and stir to combine. Set aside and let cool.

Assemble the tamales (see pages 5-6), using a heaping 1/4 cup masa, 2 to 3 tablespoons chicken mixture, 1 tablespoon crème fraîche, and a large pinch each of Swiss and Jack cheese per tamale. Transfer to a steamer and steam for 50 minutes.

Red Chile Pork Sausage Tamales

These are unbelievably simple to make using prepared enchilada sauce out of the can. They are also delicious served with the Super Easy Red Pasilla Chile Sauce. MAKES 8 TAMALES

2 cups Basic Fresh Masa (page 21)

2 (8-ounce) packages pork sausage links, raw (turkey sausage can be used if preferred)

1 (15-ounce) can prepared enchilada sauce or 2 cups Super Easy Red Pasilla Chile Sauce (page 36)

Assemble the tamales (see pages 5-6) using $1/4$ cup masa, 2 sausage links, and 2 heaping tablespoons sauce for each tamale. Transfer to a steamer and steam for 55 minutes.

Red Chile Beef Tamales

This is one of the more traditional Mexican tamales. The canned beef and canned sauce make this an easy version of the classic dish.

MAKES 18 TO 24 TAMALES

4 or 5 (12-ounce) cans roast beef

3 tablespoons olive oil

$1/4$ cup chile paste, store-bought or homemade (page 34)

1 (28-ounce) can enchilada sauce

1 teaspoon ground cumin

1 teaspoon oregano

2 teaspoons sugar

$4^{1}/_{2}$ to 6 cups Basic Fresh Masa (page 21)

1 (16-ounce) can whole pitted black olives

Open the cans of roast beef into a strainer placed over a bowl. (If the roast beef is dry, omit this step.) Save the gravy for another use or discard. Heat the olive oil in a medium sauté pan over medium heat. Stir in the chile paste and sauté until heated through, 2 to 3 minutes. Add the enchilada sauce, cumin, oregano, and sugar, stir to combine, and cook for about 10 minutes, or until bubbly. Add the strained meat and cook for 5 more minutes. Place in a bowl and let cool.

Assemble the tamales (see pages 5-6), using $1/4$ cup masa, $1/4$ cup meat, 1 heaping tablespoon sauce, and 2 or 3 olives, placed on top of the meat and sauce, for each tamale. Transfer to a steamer and steam for 1 hour.

Refried Bean and Chorizo Tamales

This is my mother's refried bean and chorizo recipe, and I've been making it on and off for as long as I can remember. It's equally good on its own as it is in tamales. To make a vegan tamale, omit the cheese and use Vegan Masa (page 26) and Soyrizo instead of regular chorizo. MAKES 18 TAMALES

2 cups prepared or
1 (15-ounce) can pinto beans

3 tablespoons butter, bacon grease, lard, or oil

12 ounces chorizo

3 green onions, chopped

1 cup grated Jack cheese, fontina, or Cheddar

3 cups Basic Fresh Masa (page 21)

If using canned beans, rinse them well and drain. Heat the butter in a 3-quart sauté pan over medium heat until sizzling, then add the beans and fry them well, mixing and mashing the beans. In a separate pan over medium heat, fry the chorizo, breaking it down with a wooden spoon, until simmering, 5 to 8 minutes. Add the beans and cook, stirring, for a minute or two, until flavors are well combined. Add the green onions and cheese and cook until the cheese is melted, about 5 minutes, stirring frequently. Set aside to cool completely.

Assemble the tamales (see pages 5-6), using $1/4$ cup masa and 2 heaping tablespoons filling for each tamale. Transfer to a steamer and steam for 50 minutes.

Albóndiga Meat Tamales

My mother taught me to make good albóndiga soup. The seasonings make the meat delicious, so it's a good choice for a tamale filling. The recipe seems complicated only because of all the ingredients, but it's really quite simple. Albóndiga is the specific name for meatball or fishball. The word originates from *albondigón*, which means "hamburger." MAKES 18 TAMALES

$\frac{1}{4}$ cup olive oil

$\frac{1}{2}$ medium or 1 small onion, diced

1 large or 2 medium ribs celery, diced

1 pound ground sirloin, pork, or veal

3 medium to large heirloom tomatoes, roughly chopped

1 small to medium potato, peeled and diced

1 teaspoon seasoned salt

$\frac{1}{2}$ teaspoon garlic powder

1 teaspoon dried oregano

Good pinch of cumin powder

$\frac{1}{2}$ teaspoon pepper

1 to $1\frac{1}{2}$ cups water or beef, chicken, or vegetable stock

2 large sprigs fresh mint, left whole, or 2 teaspoons dried

$4\frac{1}{2}$ cups Basic Fresh Masa (page 21)

In a large sauté pan over medium heat, heat the oil, add the onion and celery, and sauté for 2 to 3 minutes. Add the ground meat, breaking it apart with a wooden spoon or spatula, and cook 2 to 3 minutes more. Add the tomatoes, potato, seasoned salt, garlic powder, oregano, cumin, and pepper and cook 2 to 3 minutes more.

Add the water and the mint. If using fresh mint, push the mint down into the liquid and cover and simmer over medium-low heat for 20 to 25 minutes, until half the liquid has been absorbed. Check and stir frequently and add more water or broth if needed. Set aside to cool. Remove the mint and discard. When cool, pour into a bowl.

Assemble the tamales (see pages 5-6), using $\frac{1}{4}$ cup masa and $\frac{1}{4}$ cup meat filling for each tamale. Transfer to a steamer and steam for 50 minutes.

Sirloin Beef Tamales

My sister, Diane, added this tamale to the menu at Tamara's Tamales years ago, because she wanted to sell a tamale made with flavored masa. In this case, the masa is flavored with Super Easy Red Pasilla Chile Sauce, which tints the masa reddish-orange in addition to flavoring it. Many Latin cooks use this idea of flavoring the masa. You can flavor any of the savory masas in the other recipes in this book. MAKES 12 TAMALES

1 pound beef sirloin

3 tablespoons olive oil

Pinch of salt

Pinch of pepper

1 small to medium onion, chopped

2 large cloves garlic, chopped

2 cups plus 6 tablespoons Super Easy Red Pasilla Chile Sauce (page 36), or 1 (28-ounce) can Las Palmas Red Chile Sauce

3 cups Basic Fresh Masa (page 21)

Cut the sirloin into 1-inch pieces. Heat the olive oil in a medium sauté pan over medium heat. Add the sirloin and salt and pepper and sauté until barely brown, or approximately 5 minutes, then add the onion and garlic and cook 5 minutes more, until the onion is translucent. Add 2 cups of the red chile sauce and cook, stirring, for 10 minutes. Set aside to cool.

Add the remaining 6 tablespoons chile sauce to the masa and mix thoroughly until well incorporated.

Assemble the tamales (see pages 5-6), using $1/4$ cup masa and $1/4$ cup filling for each tamale. Transfer to a steamer and steam for 50 minutes.

Chorizo Corundas

These corundas will be a sure hit with this simple, stress-free preparation. They make a perfect meal or snack. If you have prepared your masa ahead of time, these can be a go-to tamale recipe for the approximately 40 minutes they take to assemble. MAKES 12 CORUNDAS

1 pound chorizo, casing removed

1 cup grated Cheddar or Jack cheese

2 cups Basic Fresh Masa (page 21)

In a medium sauté pan over medium heat, fry the chorizo until barely cooked and melted down, mashing it down with a large fork or wooden spoon, 7 to 8 minutes. Set aside and allow to cool.

Mix together the chorizo, cheese, and masa in a medium bowl until well combined.

Assemble the corundas (see page 8), using $1/4$ cup for each corunda. Transfer to a steamer and steam for 50 minutes.

Chorizo and Egg Tamales

The combination of chorizo and eggs is a staple Mexican breakfast item. Why not make tamales with these especially easy ingredients?

MAKES 12 TAMALES

1 pound chorizo sausage, casing removed

1 small onion, chopped

6 eggs, beaten

Pinch of dried oregano

3 cups Basic Fresh Masa (page 21)

Heat the chorizo sausage in a medium skillet over medium heat, breaking it up with a wooden spoon as it gently cooks and melts down, 7 to 8 minutes. Add the onion and cook for 2 minutes more. Do not overcook—it should be moist and not dry. Add the eggs and oregano and continue to cook, stirring, for a few minutes, until the eggs are barely done and resemble scrambled eggs. Set aside to cool.

Assemble the tamales (see pages 5-6), using $^1/_4$ cup masa and 2 heaping tablespoons for each tamale. Transfer to a steamer and steam for 50 minutes.

Nose-to-Tail Tamales

THIS IS MY FAVORITE CHAPTER. I consider myself fortunate to have had grandparents who introduced us to eating and enjoying so many different parts of meat, poultry, and fish, I grew up loving these "extraordinary" ingredients, and, of course, I learned to cook them all. For the most part, they are straightforward and extremely simple to cook.

If you love to eat different parts of the animal or are an adventurous eater, then you will love these recipes. If you have not tried these meats, then I am sure that within these pages you will find interesting recipes to spark your sense of adventure. I promise you, they're delicious!

For many years I had wanted to roast a whole pig or lamb in a pit in the ground. I talked my family into doing it at my father's house for my brother Stephen's visit from Connecticut. The men dug the hole and lined it with bricks and stones, started the wood fire on top of the stones, and waited to get the embers. Meanwhile, the women prepared the meats; we had decided that now that we were finally going to attempt it, we might as well go all-out. We prepared a pig, a whole turkey, a huge roast of goat, a leg of lamb, and a giant whole tuna. Each one was all dressed, spiced, and wrapped individually in foil, banana leaves, and gunny sacks. We placed them in the hole with the embers, then covered the hole with banana leaves, wire mesh, and dirt. Five hours later, we dug it up and had a feast with family, friends, and neighbors. All the meats were filled with intense flavor and fall-off-the-bone tender. It is always a unique experience to cook and eat the whole animal. It has a primal, honoring-of-traditions feel to it.

Beef Cheeks and Wine Tamales

For me, beef cheeks are simple and sublime, and this recipe makes them so. It is almost like making stew or an easy version of boeuf bourguignon. Make this even simpler by using a slow cooker or pressure cooker.

MAKES 30 TAMALES

1/4 cup olive oil

2 pounds beef cheeks, cut into 2-inch pieces, seasoned with salt and pepper

4 medium onions, chopped

3 tablespoons flour (use rice flour if gluten free)

1 cup red wine

5 large carrots, cut into 1/2-inch slices

2 cloves garlic

1 tablespoon fresh parsley

1 tablespoon fresh thyme

1 tablespoon fresh oregano

1 teaspoon dried marjoram

2 or 3 bay leaves

1 tablespoon Kitchen Bouquet or Maggi sauce

8 cups Basic Fresh Masa (page 21)

In a large frying pan or heavy pot, heat the olive oil over high heat and brown the beef in batches (each batch should take 5 to 7 minutes); set aside. Turn down the heat to medium, add the onions, and cook for 5 to 8 minutes, until soft and golden, scraping the bits off the bottom of the pan as they loosen. Add the flour, stirring and cooking for a few more minutes. Add the wine, finish scraping all the bits and cooked meat juices off the bottom of the pan, and bring to a gentle boil.

Add the browned beef, carrots, garlic, herbs, Kitchen Bouquet or Maggi sauce, and enough water to cover. Return to a boil over medium-high heat, and then reduce the heat to low and simmer for 2 hours, or until fork-tender. Or cover the pot and place in a 325°F oven for 2 hours, until fork-tender. Check and stir often, and add water a little at a time, if needed. Remove and discard the bay leaves. Allow to cool completely.

Assemble the tamales (see pages 5-6), using 1/4 cup masa and 1/4 cup filling for each tamale. Transfer to a steamer and steam for 55 minutes.

Beef or Pork Blood Tamales

These are probably my favorite tamales in the book. They're good served with eggs or potatoes or fantastic all by themselves. To save time, you can make one large tamale instead of traditional small ones. When done, serve immediately, or cut it into slices after it cools and fry it as you would blood sausage. Korean, Filipino, and Chinese markets carry beef and pork blood in small plastic tubs in the freezer section. I prefer using beef blood, because it has a richer flavor. Pork blood usually has water added to it. MAKES 6 INDIVIDUAL TAMALES OR 1 LARGE TAMALE

³/₄ to 1 cup beef or pork blood

¹/₂ small onion, chopped

1 to 2 tablespoons oil

1 cup Basic Fresh Masa (page 21)

Good pinch of salt

Good pinch of pepper

¹/₈ teaspoon marjoram

¹/₈ teaspoon allspice

¹/₄ teaspoon thyme

1 or 2 bay leaves, crumbled

¹/₄ to ¹/₂ cup ground pork

¹/₄ to ¹/₂ cup pork fatback, chopped or minced

Remove the blood from the freezer and let it defrost (this happens pretty quickly). Meanwhile, in a medium sauté pan over medium-high heat, sauté the onion in the oil until translucent, about 5 minutes. Set aside to cool. Place the masa in a medium bowl and add the blood, sautéed onion, salt and pepper, and all the spices and mix well. Fold in the raw ground pork and then the fat.

Using all of the prepared blood masa, assemble approximately 6 tamales (see pages 5-6), using a heaping ¹/₄ cup masa for each, or make one large tamale, placing all the masa in the center of a 12 by 12-inch banana leaf and forming it into a long rectangle, resembling a fat sausage, and then tying. Transfer to a steamer and steam for about 55 minutes for the smaller tamales or 1 hour and 15 minutes for the large one.

Blood Sausage Tamales

Made with prepared blood sausage, these are easy and delicious. If you prefer to make your own blood sausage, which is what I do, by all means do so. If using prepared sausage, I prefer German, French, or Irish blood sausages for the spices and flavors. MAKES 6 TAMALES

1 pound prepared blood sausage

$^3/_4$ teaspoon spice mixture of dried marjoram, thyme, and crushed bay leaf (optional)

2 to 3 cups Basic Fresh Masa (page 21)

Take the casing off the blood sausage. If the sausage is 1 inch thick, slice it lengthwise in half and then into 4-inch strips. If the sausage is 2 inches thick, slice it lengthwise into quarters and then into 4-inch strips, or cut it into six equal pieces.

Spanish or Mexican sausages are flavored with chile, onion, and garlic, so if that is what you have, sprinkle $^1/_8$ teaspoon of the spice mixture over the sausage for each tamale.

Assemble the tamales (see pages 5-6), using $^1/_4$ or $^1/_2$ cup masa and one piece of blood sausage for each tamale. Transfer to a steamer and steam for 45 to 50 minutes.

Bone Marrow Tamales or Corundas

Bone marrow is such a treat and amazing in tamales. The rich, fatty, beefy flavor is irresistible. MAKES 4 TO 6 SMALL TAMALES OR CORUNDAS

1 to 2 pounds marrow bones

$^1/_2$ to $^3/_4$ cup Basic Fresh Masa (page 21)

Salt and pepper

Scoop out the marrow from the bones and place on a plate. The marrow will break up quite a bit as you scoop it out. Discard the bones.

To make tamales, divide the marrow into 4 to 6 portions. Using your hands and squeezing very tightly, form each portion of marrow into a 1 by 4-inch rectangle. Wrap each piece in plastic wrap and freeze until solid; this keeps it from dissolving into the masa during the steaming process.

When ready to cook, take the marrow out of the freezer and unwrap each piece. Using the largest corn husks, thinly spread 2 tablespoons masa onto the husk and place the still-frozen marrow piece in the center. Add a pinch of salt and pepper and fold over and up. Transfer to a steamer and steam the tamales immediately for 35 minutes.

To make corundas, add salt and pepper to the marrow and spread on a plate in one layer, taking care not to break it up, then place in the freezer. When the marrow is completely frozen, gently fold it into the masa until combined. You want to be careful not to break down the marrow because it should remain chunky during the steaming process. Assemble 4 to 6 corundas (see page 8), using $^1/_4$ cup masa for each one. Transfer to a steamer and steam for 40 to 45 minutes.

Pigtail Tamales

Pigtails are delicious and underappreciated, and this recipe truly puts the "tail" in "nose to tail"! Here, as with most of the recipes in this chapter, you will be using everything except the bones. It takes time to steam the tails, but most of it is unattended. MAKES 18 TAMALES

3 to $3^{1}/_{2}$ pounds pork tails, rinsed well

$^{1}/_{2}$ onion, chopped

1 (7-ounce) can chopped or whole green chiles, or 2 or 3 fresh jalapeños, seeded and chopped

1 small potato, diced

$^{1}/_{8}$ teaspoon seasoned salt

$^{1}/_{8}$ teaspoon freshly ground pepper

1 cup chicken stock

$4^{1}/_{2}$ cups Basic Fresh Masa (page 21)

In a large steaming pot, fill the bottom with water and place the pigtails into the basket above the water level. Sprinkle with salt and pepper to taste. Steam the pigtails over medium-high heat for $3^{1}/_{2}$ to 4 hours. Check the water frequently to keep the water level high, each time discarding the water and adding clean boiling water to the pot (this discards unwanted fat, ensuring a leaner meat). When the meat is falling off the bones, transfer the tails to a plate and allow to cool.

When cool enough to handle, remove all the meat, skin, and any remaining fat from the bones. Discard the bones. Place the meat into a sauté pan, add the onion, chiles, potato, salt, pepper, and stock, then cover and cook over medium heat for 10 to 15 minutes or until the potatoes are soft. Place into a bowl and allow to cool, or refrigerate until ready to make tamales.

Assemble the tamales (see pages 5-6) using a $^{1}/_{4}$ cup masa and $^{1}/_{4}$ cup filling for each tamale. Transfer to a steamer and steam for 55 minutes.

Lamb Head Tamales

I learned to make lamb heads from my grandfather, who made them once a week. They were cheap and very accessible to buy, and the meat on the head is very delicious. I make lamb heads at least half a dozen times a year. They are worth making the effort to find and cook. You can also find a restaurant that makes them, such as Prune in New York City. Call first to make sure they have them. Or ask your butcher to order them for you, or go to a Hispanic market or a restaurant supply store. They usually come split right down the middle; if they are whole, have them split. The meat closest to the bone is the most flavorful. MAKES 12 TAMALES

1 (4- to 4¹/₄-pound) lamb head, cut in half lengthwise

Garlic salt

Pepper

1 to 2 tablespoons butter

1 to 2 tablespoons flour (use rice flour if gluten free)

1 (16-ounce) can beef broth

2 to 3 cups Basic Fresh Masa (page 21)

Preheat the oven to 350°F. Generously sprinkle the head halves with the garlic salt and pepper. Lay flat-side down in a large roasting pan. Roast for 2 hours, or until brown and crispy. Set aside to cool.

Take the two halves of the head off the roasting pan. Set the pan aside. Remove all the meat, brains, tongue, eyes, and crispy parts. Remove the skin from the tongue, then roughly chop all of it together. This will be difficult to do without eating a good amount of it. Set aside.

In a small skillet over medium heat, melt the butter. Add the flour and whisk until the mixture turns slightly brown and foamy, 4 to 5 minutes. Set the roux aside.

Place the roasting pan on the stove over two burners set to medium heat. Add the beef broth and scrape up all the bits from the bottom of the pan with a spatula. As the broth heats, the bits and pieces will scrape off easily. When all of the bits are incorporated into the broth, add the roux and heat until thickened into a nice gravy. Taste for salt, but most likely, if you seasoned the heads at the beginning well enough, the gravy will be perfect. Pour into a bowl. Set aside to cool.

Assemble the tamales (see pages 5-6), using 2 heaping tablespoons masa, $1/4$ cup meat filling, and 2 tablespoons gravy for each tamale. Transfer to a steamer and steam for 50 minutes.

Chicharrónes and New Mexico Green Chile Tamales

New Mexico green chile is a real treat. I used to go all the way to Hatch, New Mexico, during the green chile season to stock up, but now a few of our local supermarkets here in Los Angeles carry them. I buy 20 to 40 pounds, pack some into bags in the freezer, roast them on the barbecue, clean them, and make jars of sauce so I can have a good supply for the year. This recipe is very spicy. If you like a milder tamale, use Anaheim chiles instead (the chiles with the round bottoms are the milder ones). Buy your pork rinds or chicharrónes at Hispanic or Mexican stores. They are a whole different thing than commercially packaged pork rinds—denser and meatier with huge flavor. MAKES 10 TAMALES

1 small onion, minced

2 cloves garlic, minced

2 carrots, minced

$^1/_4$ cup olive oil, butter, or margarine

10 fresh New Mexico (Hatch) chiles, roasted, cleaned, and finely chopped

1 to 2 cups chicken broth

$^1/_4$ teaspoon salt

4 ounces prepared (prefried) pork rinds (chicharrónes)

$2^1/_2$ cups Basic Fresh Masa (page 21)

In a medium frying pan or saucepan over medium heat, sauté the onion, garlic, and carrots in the oil until soft, about 5 minutes. Add the chiles, 1 cup of the chicken broth, and salt, cover, and simmer for $1^1/_2$ hours, checking and stirring often and adding more broth as needed. You want a soupy consistency.

Add the pork rinds and stir to combine. Cover and continue cooking for 15 minutes longer, or until the pork rinds are soft. Set aside to cool.

Assemble the tamales (see pages 5-6), using $^1/_4$ cup masa and 2 heaping tablespoons filling with sauce for each tamale. Transfer to a steamer and steam for 50 minutes.

Tongue Tamales

Tongue, when made correctly, melts in your mouth—it's extremely flavorful, has a buttery texture, and is a delicious part of the animal to eat. I grew up eating tongue at least once a month. I once served this tongue recipe (the meat only, not the tamales), told my guests it was a roast, and because it was all cut up they didn't know the difference. They loved it! I told them it was tongue afterward and we all had a good laugh.

MAKES 12 TO 18 TAMALES

3 to 3^1/$_2$ pounds beef tongue

1 medium onion, halved

3 large cloves garlic

Salt and pepper

1 teaspoon garlic powder

2 teaspoons crushed oregano

2 tablespoons butter

2 tablespoons flour

1 fresh serrano chile, seeded and minced

^{1}/$_4$ cup dry sherry or Madeira wine

3 to 4^1/$_2$ cups Basic Fresh Masa (page 21)

Rinse the tongue well with cold water and place in a Dutch oven or large pot with the onion and garlic. Cover with water and add salt and pepper to taste. Cook over medium heat for 1^1/$_2$ to 2 hours, or until it is tender enough to easily stick a fork or knife in it. Check the water level and add more if needed. Transfer to a large platter and let cool, reserving the stock in the pot. When it is cool enough to handle, remove all the skin and discard.

Preheat the oven to 350°F. Cut the tongue into ^{1}/$_4$-inch slices and arrange on a slightly oiled cookie sheet. Sprinkle with the garlic powder and oregano. Bake for 20 to 25 minutes, until slightly browned. Remove from the oven and let cool.

In a small skillet over medium heat, melt the butter. Add the flour and whisk until the mixture turns slightly brown and foamy, 4 to 5 minutes. Set the roux aside.

While the tongue is baking, boil down the stock until you have about 2 cups left in the pot. Add the roux, chile, and sherry. Cook, stirring, until it thickens, and then cook for about 5 minutes more. Cut the tongue into 1-inch cubes and add to the gravy. Let cool.

Assemble the tamales (see pages 5-6), using $1/4$ cup masa and $1/4$ cup filling per tamale, distributing all the gravy with the meat. Transfer to a steamer and steam for 55 minutes.

Oxtail Tamales

Oxtails are a staple food in my family and are common in Cuban, Jamaican, Mexican, French, English, and Spanish home cooking. Many cooks use pressure cookers or slow cookers to cook them faster. Most supermarkets sell oxtails, but if you don't see them in the meat case, ask the butcher.

MAKES 10 TO 12 TAMALES

2 tablespoons olive oil

3 pounds oxtails, trimmed of some fat (at least half)

1 medium onion, chopped

4 large cloves garlic, sliced

2 large ribs celery, chopped

1 large tomato, chopped, or 1 (6-ounce) can tomato paste or tomato sauce

2 cups beef stock

2 cups water, plus more if needed

2 tablespoons beef bouillon

2 tablespoons freshly grated allspice

2 tablespoons crushed red chile (chile quebrado)

1 teaspoon freshly ground pepper

$2^{1}/_{2}$ to 3 cups Basic Fresh Masa (page 21)

Heat the oil in a Dutch oven or large pot over medium-high heat. Add the oxtails and brown on all sides, 15 to 20 minutes. Remove the oxtails to a plate. Add the onion, garlic, and celery to the pot and sauté until soft, about 3 minutes. Add the tomato, stock, water, bouillon, and spices and stir to combine. Add the oxtails back to the pot, cover, and simmer for 4 to $4^{1}/_{2}$ hours, until the meat comes easily away from the bone. Check often to add water, 1 cup at a time, if needed.

Remove the oxtails from the pot and place on a plate to cool. When cool, remove all the meat from the bones and set aside. Discard the bones. Pour the gravy into a bowl and place in the freezer for about 45 minutes, or until all the fat has formed a layer on top. With a large spoon or spatula, scrape off all the fat and discard, then mix the meat into the gravy. Taste and adjust flavor the seasoning.

Assemble the tamales (see pages 5-6), using $^{1}/_{4}$ cup masa and $^{1}/_{4}$ cup filling for each tamale. Transfer to a steamer and steam for 55 minutes.

Tripe Tamales

Tripe is the stomach lining of beef, pork, and other animals. It is eaten all over the world, and in Mexico and South America it is usually made into soup, or *menudo*. This recipe came from my trip to Italy. I ate tripe in Florence and then bought it in Umbria when we stayed at a farmhouse in Agriano. I have since been making the Italian version (with basil, onion, garlic, and fresh tomatoes); however, for this recipe I swapped the basil for cilantro to make more traditional tamales. If you want some spice, add chopped chiles to taste. MAKES 12 TO 18 TAMALES

2 pounds tripe

1 lemon

8 cups water

1 large onion, halved

5 or 6 large cloves garlic

2 to 3^1/$_2$ teaspoons salt

^{1}/$_4$ cup olive oil

4 large tomatoes, chopped, or 1 (28-ounce) can whole tomatoes or tomato sauce

^{1}/$_2$ (6-ounce) can tomato paste

Good pinch of pepper

1 teaspoon dried oregano, finely crushed

^{1}/$_4$ to ^{1}/$_2$ bunch fresh cilantro

3 to 4^1/$_2$ cups Basic Fresh Masa (page 21)

Working on a cutting board, remove all the fat from the back of the tripe with a knife or pull it off with your fingers. Place it in a large bowl or 5-quart pot and add water to cover. Cut the lemon in half and squeeze the juice into the pot, seeds and all, then add both spent lemon halves. Let stand for 1 to 2 hours to remove any odor. The tripe I buy is so fresh it doesn't have a strong smell, but I still rinse and soak it.

When ready, dump out the water and lemon rinds and seeds and rinse the tripe well under running water. Add the 8 cups water to a 5-quart pot along with the tripe, half the onion, 4 cloves of the garlic, and 2 to 3 teaspoons of the salt. Bring to a boil over medium-high heat and cook, partially covered, for 2^1/$_2$ hours, checking to add water if needed.

Remove the tripe and place on a large plate to cool completely. Reserve 1 cup of the broth, discarding the onion and garlic. When the tripe is cool, cut into either 1-inch pieces or $1/2$ by 2-inch strips.

Heat the olive oil in a large skillet over medium heat. Chop the remaining half of the onion and mince the remaining 1 or 2 cloves garlic. Add to the skillet along with the tomatoes, tomato paste, $1/2$ teaspoon salt, the pepper, oregano, and cilantro. Add the reserved cooking broth. Cook for about 20 minutes to cook the onions and combine all the flavors. Taste the mixture for salt, adding more if you wish. Add the tripe and stir to combine.

Preheat the oven to 325°F. Transfer the tripe mixture to a 3- or 4-quart casserole dish, cover with a lid or foil, and bake for $2^1/4$ hours, until the tripe is fork-tender.

Assemble the tamales (see pages 5-6), using $1/4$ cup masa and $1/4$ cup tripe filling for each tamale. Transfer to a steamer and steam for 50 minutes.

Wild Boar Carnitas Tamales

If you are an hunting enthusiast and hunt your own boar, or know someone who does, as we do, you'll know what I mean when I say that these are amazing. A friend and customer, Mark, brought a wild boar roast into our shop—he and a group of his friends hunt wild boar in the Tejon Valley area of Bakersfield, California. I made oven boar carnitas the same way we make our regular oven pork carnitas, and they were delicious. Regular pork shoulder can be used in this recipe, but if you can get your hands on some wild boar, use that—it's delicious! The carnitas can also be made in a slow cooker or pressure cooker if you wrap the meat securely with a few layers of foil. MAKES 18 TO 24 TAMALES

5 to 7 large cloves garlic

2^1/$_2$ to 3 pounds wild boar (shoulder or picnic roast are good selections)

2 teaspoons salt

1 teaspoon pepper

3 to 3^1/$_2$ cups Super Easy Red Pasilla Chile Sauce (page 36)

4^1/$_2$ to 6 cups Basic Fresh Masa (page 21)

Preheat the oven to 325°F.

Crush the garlic and spread it all over the roast, saving any blood and juices from the meat. Season with salt and pepper and place in a casserole dish or pan. Pour the reserved blood onto the roast, then cover with two or three layers of foil, making sure it's tight around the casserole or pan. Bake for 4 to 4^1/$_2$ hours, until brown and crunchy on the outside. Set aside and let cool completely. Cut the meat into 1-inch cubes, pull it apart in small chunks, or shred it with your fingers or a fork.

Place the meat into a large bowl, pour the sauce over, and gently fold the sauce into the meat.

Assemble the tamales (see pages 5-6), using ^{1}/$_4$ cup masa and ^{1}/$_4$ cup meat filling for each tamale. Transfer to a steamer and steam for 50 to 55 minutes.

Cow's Foot Tamales

I love cow's foot stew, soup, beans, and anything else made with them. One of my favorite Jamaican restaurants makes cow's foot soup. Cow's feet have a rich, beefy flavor and are gelatinous and delicious. Sometimes, when I want the flavor of beef feet, I buy beef tendons and cook them the same way, without having to deal with the bones. Ask your butcher for them or check out Hispanic, Korean, and Chinese markets. MAKES 12 TAMALES

1 (3- to 3¹/₂-pound) cow's foot, skin removed

Juice of 2 lemons or limes

1 small whole onion

5 large cloves garlic, unpeeled

2 dried ancho or pasilla chiles, stemmed and seeded

1 to 2 tablespoons salt, or to taste

1 to 2 teaspoons pepper, or to taste

3 cups Basic Fresh Masa (page 21)

Rinse the foot well under cold water, then place it whole into an 8- to 10-quart pot and add cold water to cover. Mix the lemon juice into the water and let it stand in the sink for 30 to 45 minutes. Pour out the water and rinse the foot and the pot well. Return the foot to the clean pot, add water to cover along with the onion and garlic, and bring it to a full boil over high heat. Lower the heat to medium-high, cover, and cook for 5 to 6 hours. After 2 hours, add the chile pods, salt, and pepper and more water to cover, if needed. Then every hour or so, stir the pot and check the water level. (This can be done at a medium boil, but the timing will be much longer, up to 8 hours.)

When it's done, the bones will have separated, the tendons will be very soft and gelatinous, and most of the chiles and garlic will have dissolved into the broth. Remove the bones and tendons and place on a large plate to cool, discarding what's left of the onion and garlic. Reserve 1 cup of the broth and either save the remaining broth for soup or another use or discard. When the bones and tendons are cool enough to handle, remove everything from the bone and mix with the cooled reserved broth. Taste and add salt if needed.

Assemble the tamales (see pages 5-6), using $^1/_4$ cup masa and 2 heaping tablespoons filling for each tamale. Transfer to a steamer and steam for 45 minutes.

Vegetarian and Vegan Tamales

SINCE OPENING OUR DOORS at Tamara's Tamales eighteen years ago, we have had both vegetarian and vegan tamales on the menu. They are some of our most popular.

Included here is an excellent variety of vegetarian and vegan tamales. My favorites are Super Easy Onion and Cheese (page 102), Pasilla Rajas (page 99), and Easy Green Corn (page 98). The Easy Green Corn is a recipe I have simplified from the traditional labor-intensive and time-consuming preparation and is just as delicious. I suggest you try all of the recipes, whether or not you are vegetarian or vegan.

Huevos Rancheros–Inspired Tamales

Ranchero eggs are a staple Mexican dish, usually made with poached eggs, smothered in a tomato-based chile sauce, and sprinkled with cheese. You can use whatever you have on hand to make the sauce, adding fresh or dried herbs, or fresh or canned chiles. I prefer using mild chiles and sometimes mix it up with a good pinch of dried oregano, thyme, or cumin. Another good option is to use canned ranchera sauce (Herdez is a great brand)— just make sure the amount of the sauce adds up to 10 to 14 ounces.

MAKES 12 TAMALES

4 or 5 green onions, chopped, or 1 small to medium onion

1 to 1^1/$_2$ tablespoons olive oil

1 (10- to 14-ounce) can tomato sauce, puree, or diced or whole tomatoes, or 3 large fresh tomatoes

1 (4-ounce) can chopped or diced green chiles, or minced fresh jalapeño or serrano chiles to taste

^{1}/$_2$ teaspoon seasoned salt

^{1}/$_2$ teaspoon pepper

Good pinch of sugar, if needed

3 cups Basic Fresh Masa (page 21)

12 eggs, hard-boiled, peeled, and halved

1 to 1^1/$_2$ cups grated Cheddar cheese

In a skillet over medium heat, sauté the onions in the olive oil for 1 to 2 minutes until soft. Add the tomato sauce, chiles, salt, and pepper and cook gently for 10 to 15 minutes. Taste the sauce; if it is a little bitter or sour, add a good pinch of sugar and cook for a few minutes more.

Assemble the tamales (see pages 5-6), using ^{1}/$_4$ cup masa, 2 halves of an egg, a good pinch of the cheese, and 2 heaping tablespoons to ^{1}/$_4$ cup sauce for each tamale. Transfer to a steamer and steam for 50 minutes.

Simple Veggie Tamales

Many Latino cooks use canned vegetable mixes for various stews, soups, and salads. If you buy Mexican vegetable tamales, they are usually made with these canned vegetables and cheese. I've punched them up a bit with canned chiles and spices. Eliminate the cheese and use Vegan Masa (page 26) to make these a vegan dish. MAKES 8 TAMALES

1 (15-ounce) can mixed vegetables, or 2 cups frozen mixed vegetables

1 cup grated Colby, Jack, or Cheddar cheese

$^1/_2$ cup canned chopped Ortega green chiles

$^1/_2$ cup chopped fresh cilantro, or 1 teaspoon dried

2 tablespoons minced fresh oregano, or $^1/_2$ teaspoon dried

$^1/_4$ teaspoon seasoned salt or plain salt

$^1/_4$ teaspoon freshly ground pepper

2 cups Basic Fresh Masa (page 21)

In a medium bowl combine all of the ingredients except the masa.

Assemble the tamales (see pages 5-6), using $^1/_4$ cup masa and $^1/_4$ cup filling for each tamale. Transfer to a steamer and steam for 55 minutes.

Calabazita Tamales

These tamales have been on our menu at Tamara's Tamales for years now. The recipe is an age-old staple of Mexican cooks. For the easier raw ingredient version, omit sautéing the vegetables, mix together all of the ingredients except the masa in a bowl, and assemble the tamales. The vegetables will cook in the steamer. MAKES 18 TAMALES

5 tablespoons olive oil

1 small onion, chopped

1 clove garlic, minced

3 medium zucchini, chopped

2 tomatoes, chopped

1 teaspoon seasoned salt

1/4 teaspoon pepper

1 cup fresh or frozen white corn

1 cup grated Jack or Cheddar cheese

4 1/2 cups Basic Fresh Masa (page 21)

In a medium sauté pan over medium-high heat, add the olive oil and sauté the onion and garlic for a few minutes, stirring often. Add the zucchini, tomatoes, salt, and pepper and cook, stirring occasionally, until the zucchini is soft, 15 to 20 minutes. Set aside and let cool completely.

Place the cooled zucchini mixture in a large bowl, add the corn and cheese, and mix well.

Assemble the tamales (see pages 5-6), using 1/4 cup masa and 1/4 cup filling for each tamale. Transfer to a steamer and steam for 50 minutes.

Artichoke Tamales

I'm sure many of you are familiar with warm artichoke dip. Well, it's absolutely delicious in a tamale! MAKES 18 TAMALES

1 (8-ounce) package cream cheese, softened

1 cup sour cream or Mexican crema

$^3/_4$ cup mayonnaise

1 teaspoon granulated garlic powder

$^1/_2$ teaspoon pepper

$^3/_4$ cup freshly grated Romano or finely crumbled Cotija cheese

1 (14-ounce) can artichokes hearts in water, well drained and quartered

$4^1/_2$ cups Basic Fresh Masa (page 21)

Preheat the oven to 350°F and grease an 8 by 8-inch casserole dish.

In a medium bowl, cream the cream cheese with a wooden spoon, and then add the sour cream and mayonnaise and whip well. Add the garlic powder and pepper and mix well. Fold in the Romano cheese and artichokes until well blended. Scrape the mixture into the casserole dish and bake for $1^1/_2$ hours. Allow to cool completely before assembling the tamales.

Assemble the tamales (see pages 5-6), using $^1/_4$ cup masa and $^1/_4$ cup filling for each tamale. Transfer to a steamer and steam for 55 minutes.

Creamy Mushroom Tamales

Mushrooms and cream? Always an excellent combination. This recipe is easy and great for mushroom lovers. MAKES 12 TAMALES

3 tablespoons unsalted butter

1 pound mixed portobello, cremini, and shiitake mushrooms, coarsely chopped

1 (6-ounce) tub crème fraîche, or ³/₄ cup sour cream

¹/₈ teaspoon garlic powder

¹/₂ teaspoon salt

¹/₄ teaspoon pepper

Milk or light cream, as needed

3 cups Basic Fresh Masa (page 21), mixed with 3 to 4 tablespoons mushroom powder (see page 26) if desired

Melt the butter in an 8-cup skillet over medium-high heat, add the mushrooms, and sauté for a few minutes, stirring often. Add the crème fraîche, garlic powder, salt, and pepper and sauté to blend the flavors, 5 to 7 minutes. Add a little milk or light cream if the mixture thickens too much; this needs to be saucy. Set aside to cool.

Assemble the tamales (see pages 5-6), using ¹/₄ cup masa and ¹/₄ cup filling for each tamale. Transfer to a steamer and steam for 50 minutes.

Easy Green Corn Tamales

This is an easy version of a tamale we make at Tamara's Tamales. You will be very pleased with the results. Because we use fresh corn husks, rather than dried, the tamales retain the green color of the husk. White dent corn is seasonal and traditionally used, and it's what we use at the shop. However, I have adapted the recipe to use the always-available regular corn on the cob from any market or farmers' market. MAKES 24 TAMALES

12 ears white or yellow corn

$1/2$ cup yellow cornmeal

$1/2$ cup unsalted butter or margarine

$1/4$ cup sugar

$1/4$ cup half-and-half

1 teaspoon salt

1 pound Cheddar cheese, cut into 24 ($1/2$ by 3-inch) slices approximately

2 (7-ounce) cans mild green chiles, cut or pulled into 24 strips

Cut about $1^1/2$ inches off the bottom of each corn cob, so the husks peel off easily. Remove all the husks carefully to keep each leaf whole to be used to wrap and assemble the tamales in place of the usual dried corn husks. Set aside. Cut the kernels off each cob and place in a food processor. Add the cornmeal and blend until smooth. Add the butter, sugar, half-and-half, and salt, blend again, and taste. Add more salt if needed.

Assemble the tamales (see pages 5-6), using 2 or 3 corn husks, $1/4$ cup corn mixture, 1 strip of cheese, and 1 strip of chile for each tamale. Wrap each tamale using the fresh corn husks and tie with strips made from the husk or wrap in parchment paper to hold it together. Transfer to a steamer and steam for 45 minutes.

Pasilla Rajas Tamales

This is my sister Diane's recipe that we sell thousands of at Tamara's Tamales. They're delicious and simple. Want to make a vegan version? Eliminate the cheeses and use Vegan Masa (page 26). MAKES 12 TAMALES

8 large fresh pasilla chiles, roasted, seeded, and deveined

$^1/_4$ cup olive oil

2 or 3 tomatoes, cut into $^1/_4$-inch slices

1 large onion, cut into $^1/_4$-inch slices

3 cloves garlic, minced

1 cup grated Jack cheese

1 cup grated Cheddar cheese

3 cups Basic Fresh Masa (page 21)

Cut each chile in half and then lengthwise into $^1/_4$-inch slices. Heat the olive oil in a skillet over medium heat, add the tomatoes, onion, and garlic, and sauté until the onions are translucent, about 5 minutes. Add the chiles and sauté for an additional 5 minutes. Turn off the heat and sprinkle with the cheeses. Cover the pan and let stand until the cheese is melted, 8 to 10 minutes. Set aside to cool completely.

Assemble the tamales (see pages 5-6), using $^1/_4$ cup masa and $^1/_4$ cup filling for each tamale. Transfer to a steamer and steam for 50 minutes.

Fresh Poblano and Potato Tamales

For convenience and ease, you can find poblano chiles already roasted and seeded in 28-ounce cans, or you can use two 7-ounce cans of Ortega brand chopped, whole, or sliced as a substitute. MAKES 12 TAMALES

$\frac{1}{2}$ cup olive oil

1 medium onion, minced

1 clove garlic, minced

2 potatoes, diced into $\frac{1}{2}$- to $\frac{1}{4}$-inch cubes

4 fresh poblano chiles, roasted or grilled, deveined, seeded, and cut into $\frac{1}{2}$-inch cubes

1 teaspoon salt

$\frac{1}{2}$ teaspoon pepper

4 cups Vegan Masa (page 26)

Heat the olive oil in 12-cup pan over medium heat. Add the onion and sauté for 20 minutes, until very soft, then add the garlic and potatoes. Stir to combine and cook for about 15 minutes, until the potatoes are almost done but still firm, stirring often. Add the chiles, salt, and pepper and continue cooking for 10 minutes, or until the flavors are melded. Taste and adjust the salt and pepper if needed. Set aside to cool.

Assemble the tamales (see pages 5-6), using $\frac{1}{3}$ cup masa and $\frac{1}{3}$ cup potato filling for each tamale. Transfer to a steamer and steam for 50 minutes to 1 hour.

Super Easy Onion and Cheese Tamales

The idea for this filling is from a quiche recipe that my sister-in-law, Jilaine, gave me years ago. It's excellent as a quiche and super easy and delicious in tamales. MAKES 8 TAMALES

1/4 cup olive oil

2 large onions, sliced

1/2 teaspoon garlic salt

1/2 teaspoon pepper

1 cup grated sharp Cheddar cheese

2 cups Basic Fresh Masa (page 21)

Heat the oil in a sauté pan over medium heat, add the onions, and sauté until caramelized, 30 minutes or more, stirring frequently to avoid burning. Add the salt and pepper and stir to combine. Remove from the heat and set aside to cool.

Assemble the tamales (see pages 5-6), using 1/2 cup masa, 1/4 cup onion filling, and a generous pinch of cheese for each tamale. Transfer to a steamer and steam for 45 minutes.

Tamara's Refried Bean and Jalapeño Rajas Tamales

One of our cooks, who is from Jalisco, Mexico, introduced us to this recipe. Tamara tweaked the dish and now makes them as a special for the shop. I make mine with ready-made refried beans I buy from the deli at our local Latin supermarket. If you have a good source, great; if not, canned beans will do, but you will need to refry them in oil and add some salt and pepper.

MAKES 6 TAMALES

5 tablespoons olive oil

$1/4$ to $1/2$ medium onion, or $1/4$ to $1/3$ cup chopped onion, chives, or leeks

2 cups refried beans

Salt or seasoned salt

Pepper

$1^1/2$ cups Basic Fresh Masa (page 21)

2 large fresh jalapeños, seeded and deveined if desired, each cut into 6 strips

8-ounce hunk any kind of cheese, cut into 12 ($1/2$ by 3-inch) strips

Heat the oil in a medium skillet over medium heat, add the onion, and fry until soft, 3 or 4 minutes. Add the beans and fry, stirring, 8 to 10 minutes, until nice and creamy. Taste (this is necessary because they may already have salt added) and add salt and pepper if needed. Set aside to cool completely.

Assemble the tamales (see pages 5-6), using $1/4$ cup masa, $1/4$ cup beans, 2 jalapeño strips, and 2 cheese strips on top. Transfer to a steamer and steam for 50 minutes.

Jalapeño Pesto Potato Tamales

Here is another great vegan tamale recipe from my sister, Diane. Because it's vegan, the recipe eliminates the Parmesan or Romano cheese found in most pesto recipes. This is also on our menu at Tamara's Tamales, and it keeps our vegan customers happy. It's also delicious made with carrots instead of potatoes. Cut four large carrots into strips and parboil them before assembling the tamales. MAKES 12 TAMALES

1 very large potato, any type

$^3/_4$ cup olive oil

7 fresh jalapeños, deveined and seeded

3 large cloves garlic

$^1/_4$ cup toasted pine nuts

1 bunch cilantro

$^1/_4$ teaspoon salt

3 cups Vegan Masa (page 26)

Peel and cut the potato lengthwise into $^1/_4$-inch "French fry" strips. Heat $^1/_4$ cup of the olive oil in a skillet over medium heat, add the potato, and fry until browned on all sides, about 20 minutes. Set aside to cool.

In food processor, process the jalapeños, garlic, pine nuts, cilantro, remaining $^1/_2$ cup olive oil, and salt until smooth.

Assemble the tamales (see pages 5-6), using $^1/_4$ cup masa, 4 or 5 strips of potato, and 2 heaping tablespoons jalapeño pesto for each tamale. Transfer to a steamer and steam for 50 minutes.

Vegan Sinaloa Tamales

These vegan tamales are a simple version of the traditional Chicken Sinaloa Tamales (page 56) we serve at Tamara's Tamales. The diced vegetables are assembled in the tamales raw and cook completely during steaming. This recipe is flexible, and you can substitute your favorite vegetables if you wish.

MAKES 18 TAMALES

1 medium zucchini, diced

1 medium potato, diced

1 carrot, diced

1 parsnip, diced

$^{1}/_{3}$ cup golden raisins

$^{1}/_{3}$ cup sliced green manzanilla olives (green olives stuffed with pimiento)

1 (4-ounce) can chopped Ortega chiles

4 to 5 tablespoons olive oil

1 small onion

1 teaspoon cumin

2 teaspoons dried oregano

1 teaspoon seasoned salt

1 (16-ounce) can chopped tomatoes

1 cup water

$4^{1}/_{2}$ cups Vegan Masa (page 26)

Place the zucchini, potato, carrot, and parsnip in a medium bowl. Add the raisins, olives, and chiles and mix well.

Heat the olive oil in a skillet over medium heat, add the onion, cumin, oregano, and salt, and sauté for about 5 minutes, until softened. Add the tomatoes and water. Cover and cook gently for 7 minutes to combine the flavors. Taste and add salt if needed. Set aside and let cool.

Assemble the tamales (see pages 5-6), using $^{1}/_{4}$ cup masa, $^{1}/_{4}$ cup vegetable mixture, and 2 tablespoons sauce on top for each tamale. Transfer to a steamer and steam for 1 hour.

Super Easy Savory Corundas

This recipe is fast, easy, and very adaptable. You can also add a chopped fresh tomato, $1/4$ cup tomato sauce, a very small diced potato, $1/4$ cup minced fresh cilantro, or any combination of these additional ingredients. Keep in mind that if you add additional ingredients, your yield of tamales will be slightly larger. MAKES 14 CORUNDAS

1 (1-ounce) package taco seasoning mix

$1/4$ teaspoon garlic powder

1 (4-ounce) can chopped green chiles

1 cup grated Cheddar or Jack cheese

3 cups Basic Fresh Masa (page 21)

In a medium bowl, combine all of the ingredients. If using additional ingredients, add and mix well.

Assemble the corundas (see page 8), using $1/4$ cup masa mixture for each corunda. Transfer to a steamer and steam for 50 minutes.

Broccoli Cheese Corundas

These are so unbelievably easy they may become a staple recipe for years to come. This is a great way to get children to eat their veggies! Serve with some sour cream or crema and your favorite salsa on the side.

MAKES 10 CORUNDAS

1 cup $1/2$-inch pieces broccoli

$1/2$ cup grated Cheddar, Colby, or Jack cheese

$1/4$ teaspoon salt, or to taste

$1^1/2$ cups Basic Fresh Masa (page 21)

In a medium bowl, combine the broccoli, cheese, and salt until well blended. Add the masa and mix well.

Assemble the corundas (see page 8), using $1/4$ cup masa mixture for each corunda. Transfer to a steamer and steam for 50 minutes.

Cilantro Pesto Corundas

Whipping up a batch of these corundas takes very little time and no fuss. Make them anytime, for any occasion—they'll be especially popular with cilantro lovers. You can easily double or triple this recipe.

MAKES 12 CORUNDAS

2 bunches fresh cilantro

3 tablespoons grated Romano or Parmesan cheese

3 heaping tablespoons pine nuts

5 tablespoons olive oil

2 cups Basic Fresh Masa (page 21)

Place the cilantro, cheese, pine nuts, and olive oil in a food processor and process until you have a smooth paste. Add the pesto to the masa and mix well.

Assemble the corundas (see page 8), using $1/4$ cup masa mixture for each corunda. Transfer to a steamer and steam for 50 minutes.

Dessert Tamales

THE TAMALES I LOVE to create the most are the sweet ones, mainly because they were my childhood favorite. I say "favorite" because there was one type we made: pineapple-anise with raisins. There were other variations of the pineapple-anise in those days, and other families made them, but to find a sweet tamale in the marketplace was rare.

To me, sweet tamales have a whimsical aspect to them, probably because flavors or fillings originate from my favorite childhood desserts and candy. They are, for the most part, the easiest to make. If you have favorite desserts and candy, it's likely you can make delicious sweet tamales using your favorite sweet flavors.

My favorite tamale in this section is the Bananas Foster (page 115). It's so good you might consider starting with it. However, there are many excellent recipes to choose from. Consider trying the Delicious Brownie (page 121); it's very easy and makes an excellent-tasting tamale, especially for chocolate lovers. Of course, you can use your favorite brownie recipe, especially if you prefer brownies flavored with mint, made with cream cheese or peanut butter, or any number of other variations. The important thing is that you can use your favorite recipes to make your tamales, or you can use my recipes as guidelines.

Baked Fig Tamales

Figs are one of my favorite fruits and make a great-tasting tamale. You can also cut the prep time by eliminating the baking process. MAKES 6 TAMALES

6 large fresh figs, or 12 dried, white, black, or brown figs

6 tablespoons brown sugar, if using fresh figs

2 cups boiling water, if using dried figs

1 to 1 1/2 cups Sweet Masa (page 27)

1/4 cup pine nuts

If using fresh figs, preheat the oven to 350°F. Place the fresh figs in a small baking dish and sprinkle with the brown sugar. Place in the oven and bake for 30 minutes. Set aside to cool.

If using dried figs, place the figs in a heatproof bowl, pour the boiling water over the figs, and let them soften for about 40 minutes. Set aside to cool.

Assemble the tamales (page 8), using 2 tablespoons masa, 1 baked fig or 2 dried figs, and a good pinch of pine nuts for each tamale. Transfer to a steamer and steam for 45 minutes.

Banana Nutella Tamales

A regular customer recently came into the tamale shop and asked Tamara if she would make this type of tamale. She whipped it up, and it has since become an occasional special on the menu. Feel free to use a different brand of the hazelnut chocolate spread or make your own. MAKES 12 TAMALES

1/4 cup unsalted butter

1/4 cup sugar

2 teaspoons vanilla extract

1/4 teaspoon ground cinnamon

6 large bananas, cut into 1/2-inch slices

3 cups Sweet Masa (page 27)

1 (13-ounce) jar Nutella

Melt the butter in a large saucepan, then add the sugar, vanilla, and cinnamon. Add the bananas and cook, stirring, for about 3 minutes, until the bananas are glazed. Set aside to cool.

Assemble the tamales (see pages 5-6), using 1/4 cup masa, 1/4 cup bananas, and 1 generous tablespoon Nutella for each tamale. Don't spread the Nutella over the bananas, just scoop it on top. Transfer to a steamer and steam for 50 minutes.

Bananas Foster Tamales

This is amazingly simple and makes a delicious tamale. Your family and friends will love them. MAKES 10 TAMALES

$^1/_2$ cup butter

$^1/_2$ cup light brown sugar

4 bananas, each cut on the diagonal into $^1/_2$-inch slices

$^1/_4$ cup dark rum

$2^1/_2$ cups Sweet Masa (page 27)

In an 8-cup saucepan over high heat, melt the butter and add the brown sugar. Using a whisk, slowly stir until the sauce is golden brown, 2 to 3 minutes. Add the bananas, turning to coat evenly, and continue to cook for a couple more minutes until bubbling. Add the rum and ignite with a long-handled match, then allow the flame to burn out. Cook for 1 minute more. Turn off the heat and set aside until completely cool.

Assemble the tamales (see pages 5-6), using $^1/_4$ cup masa and $^1/_4$ cup filling for each tamale, making sure you use all the sauce and distribute it evenly. Transfer to a steamer and steam for 50 minutes.

Oreo Tamales

Here the Oreos are used as the filling. These tamales are so simple, unique, and fun, and your guests will really like them. They can also be made into corundas (see page 8). Simply mix the crushed Oreos into the masa (for one 15.5-ounce package of Oreos, use about 2 cups of plain masa) and steam them for the same amount of time. They are excellent either way.
MAKES 12 TAMALES

1 (15.5-ounce) package Oreo cookies

3 cups Sweet Masa (page 27)

Crush the whole package of Oreos in a food processor until coarse crumbs are formed. Or place in a plastic bag and crush with a rolling pin.

Assemble the tamales (see pages 5-6), using $1/4$ cup masa and $1/4$ cup crushed Oreos for each tamale. Transfer to a steamer and steam for 50 minutes.

Chocolate Bread Pudding Tamales

This tamale is inspired by my son-in-law, Ty, who loves bread pudding. This bread pudding is delicious on its own, and it makes a tasty and surprising tamale filling, too. MAKES 16 TAMALES

$1/2$ cup Karo syrup, light or dark

$1^1/4$ cups chocolate chips

$1/4$ teaspoon ground cinnamon

2 eggs

$3/4$ cup half-and-half

$1/4$ cup unsalted butter, melted

7 slices stale or toasted bread, any type (I use French bread), cubed

4 cups Sweet Masa (page 27)

In a microwave-safe bowl, microwave the syrup for $1^1/2$ minutes, then stir in the chocolate chips and cinnamon. Add the eggs and half-and-half, mixing until smooth. (To do this on the stove top, place the syrup, chocolate chips, and cinnamon in a medium bowl over a saucepan of boiling water or a double boiler and stir until the chips are melted and thoroughly combined, 3 to 4 minutes. Add the half-and-half first, then the eggs, mixing until smooth.) In another bowl, pour the melted butter evenly over the bread cubes and toss until well coated. Add the bread to the chocolate mixture and let soak for 20 minutes.

Preheat the oven to 350°F and grease an 8-inch square baking pan. Pour the chocolate and bread mixture into the pan. Bake for 1 hour. Remove from the oven and let cool completely. Cut into sixteen 1 by 4-inch slices.

Assemble the tamales (see pages 5-6), using $1/4$ cup masa and 1 slice bread pudding for each tamale. Transfer to a steamer and steam for 45 minutes.

Rice Pudding Tamales

This is the only rice type of filling that I have ever made for tamales. The idea came from an article I saw in a newspaper years ago where the headline was mispunctuated—it read "Authentic Mexican Favorites—Handmade Tortillas, Rice Pudding Tamales." As I read the article, it became apparent that the comma was left out after "Rice Pudding"! This gave me the idea for rice pudding tamales. My family loves rice pudding, and I have been making it for years. If you have a favorite rice pudding recipe, all the better! MAKES 16 TAMALES

3 cups cooked rice

1 (12-ounce) can evaporated milk

$^1/_2$ cup light cream

$^1/_3$ cup sugar

$^1/_3$ cup golden raisins

2 tablespoons vanilla extract

$^1/_2$ teaspoon ground cinnamon

Good pinch of salt

4 cups Sweet Masa (page 27)

Place all of the ingredients except the masa in a medium saucepan and stir well. Bring to a boil over medium-high heat, stirring often and watching closely so it doesn't burn. Reduce the heat to very low, cover, and simmer for 5 to 7 minutes, just until the mixture thickens. It will set up firmer when it has cooled down. Set aside and allow to cool completely.

Assemble the tamales (see pages 5-6), using $^1/_4$ cup masa and $^1/_4$ cup rice pudding for each tamale. Transfer to a steamer and steam for 50 minutes.

Delicious Brownie Tamales

Brownie lovers beware—these are so good you will want to make them over and over again! Using boxed brownie mix works amazingly well here, and other prepared cake mixes can be used, too, such as red velvet, spice, carrot cake . . . there are plenty of choices. Note that the water usually called for when using a boxed mix is not used here, making the dough thick and manageable. About 1 tablespoon of the filling is used because it expands when steamed. MAKES 30 TO 36 TAMALES

1 (18-ounce or larger) box plain fudge brownie mix

1/2 cup vegetable, corn, soybean, or canola oil

2 eggs

1 cup mini or regular chocolate chips

1 cup coarsely chopped walnuts (optional)

7 1/2 to 9 cups Sweet Masa (page 27)

Combine the brownie mix, oil, and eggs in a medium bowl until well blended. Fold in the chocolate chips and walnuts until combined.

Assemble the tamales (see pages 5-6), using 1/4 cup masa and 1 heaping tablespoon brownie mixture for each tamale. Transfer to a steamer and steam for 50 minutes.

Applesauce Spice Corundas

This is a good recipe to make if you're craving something sweet but don't have a lot of ingredients on hand. As with most corundas, it's easy to mix all of the ingredients together and assemble the tamales. You can also substitute a 6-ounce jar of apple butter for the applesauce, if you wish.
MAKES 12 CORUNDAS

1 cup applesauce

$^1/_2$ teaspoon cinnamon

$^1/_8$ teaspoon mace (optional; I recommend using only if you are familiar with this spice and like the taste)

2 teaspoons vanilla

$^1/_3$ cup brown sugar

2 tablespoons apple liqueur, such as Calvados (optional)

2 cups Sweet Masa (page 27)

Strain the applesauce for several hours or overnight in a fine sieve to remove some of the moisture.

Add all of the ingredients to the masa and mix well. The consistency will be slightly runny but will firm up during the steaming process.

Assemble the corundas (see page 8), using $^1/_4$ cup masa mixture for each corunda, working quickly with the thin masa. Transfer to a steamer and steam for 45 minutes.

Lemon Curd Corundas

These have a bright, fresh taste and are very easy to make. A must-make if you love lemon! If you have your own recipe for homemade lemon curd, feel free to use that instead of the premade kind. MAKES 10 CORUNDAS

1 (10-ounce) jar lemon curd

2½ cups Sweet Masa (page 27)

Fresh lemon zest (optional)

Mix 10 heaping tablespoons of the lemon curd with the masa in a 4-cup bowl until well combined. Add the zest to taste. Assemble the corundas (see page 8), using ⅓ cup masa mixture for each corunda. Transfer to a steamer and steam for 45 minutes.

Coconut Lime Corundas

These corundas are inspired by a recipe from the *Frida's Fiestas* cookbook featuring limes stuffed with coconut, a unique and refreshing Mexican dessert. Made as a tamale, they are well flavored and make a nice dessert option. I particularly like the green tint the limes give the masa.

MAKES 6 CORUNDAS

1 cup Angel Flake coconut

2 tablespoons tequila, or to taste

$1/3$ cup sugar

Grated zest of 3 limes

1 cup Basic Fresh Masa (page 21)

In a small bowl, mix together the coconut and tequila and let soak for a few hours or up to overnight. In a large bowl, add the tequila-infused coconut, sugar, and lime zest to the masa and mix well to combine.

Assemble the corundas (see page 8), using $1/4$ cup masa mixture for each corunda. Transfer to a steamer and steam for 45 minutes.

Dulce de Leche Corundas

My aunt, Guillermina, my father's sister, made a candy for us as kids, and it is the inspiration for this recipe. If you like the taste of sweetened evaporated milk, you're going to like these corundas. MAKES 12 CORUNDAS

2 cups Basic Fresh Masa (page 21)

1 (14-ounce) can sweetened evaporated milk

1 tablespoon cornstarch

1 tablespoon vanilla extract

$^1/_2$ cup raisins

Good pinch of salt

Pinch of cinnamon (optional)

In an 8-cup bowl, combine the masa and milk. Add the cornstarch, vanilla, raisins, salt, and cinnamon and mix until well blended.

Assemble the corundas (see page 8), using $^1/_4$ or $^1/_3$ cup masa mixture for each corunda. Transfer to a steamer and steam for 45 minutes.

Quince Corundas

We had a quince tree in our backyard growing up, so we always had fresh quince jam. I still make it on occasion when quince is in season. If you make your own quince jam, you can use that here, but store-bought will still be very good. MAKES 6 CORUNDAS

3/4 cup quince jam or prepared quince paste

1/4 cup sugar

1 cup Basic Fresh Masa (page 21)

Mix all the ingredients together well in a medium bowl.

Assemble the corundas (see page 8), using 1/4 cup masa mixture for each corunda. Transfer to a steamer and steam for 1 hour.

Acknowledgments

I WOULD LIKE TO THANK MY FAMILY—Steven, Tamara, Diane, Kianna, Jahna, Tyrone, Stephen, Paula, Joe, Marianne, and Roshelle—and my friends Yvonnie, Dee Dee, Olga Rose, Mari, Sara, Petra, and Anna, for all of your love, support, and cheerful willingness to try new recipes over the years. Special thanks also to Teresa, Guillermo, Margarita, Matt, and Ty for your hard work and contribution.

Gratitude is also due to the many wonderful customers who have faithfully patronized Tamara's since we first opened nearly two decades ago—we are honored to serve you!

Thanks also to Kaitlin Ketchum, Chloe Rawlins, and Anitra Alcantara at Ten Speed Press, as well as the marketing and publicity teams at Ten Speed and The Crown Publishing Group. And many thanks to photographer Sara Remington and food stylist Christine Wolheim for making everything look so delicious.

About the Author

ALICE GUADALUPE TAPP is co-owner of Tamara's Tamales located in the Marina del Rey area of Los Angeles. Now entering its nineteenth year, it has been hailed as the first tamale shop of its kind and specializes in more than 30 varieties of tamales. Along with her daughter, Tamara, Alice brings an innovative approach to the venerable tradition of tamale making while maintaining Hispanic customs. She is the author of *Tamales 101: A Beginner's Guide to Making Traditional Tamales*, published by Ten Speed Press in 2002.

Prior to opening her tamale shop, Alice enjoyed 35 years of success in a diverse career, first working in the entertainment industry, and then running her own financial management company and consulting business. She self published her first book, *Heal Your Relationship with Money*.

As a master cook and restaurant owner, Alice currently dedicates herself to expanding her culinary knowledge to create wholesome and delicious food to share with family, friends, and customers. Sift two parts Hispanic tradition and three parts business acumen, gently folding in a lifetime of knowledge, ingenuity and a passion for food, and you have the recipe for *Tamales: Fast and Delicious Mexican Meals*.

Buen provecho!

Index

TO STEVEN AND TAMARA

Library of Congress Cataloging-in-Publication Data
Tapp, Alice Guadalupe, 1944-
  Tamales / by Alice Guadalupe Tapp.
      pages cm
  Includes index.
1. Tamales. 2. Cooking, Mexican. I. Title.
  TX836.T368 2014
  641.5972—dc23

                                    2014010391

Hardcover ISBN: 978-1-60774-596-9
eBook ISBN: 978-1-60774-597-6

Printed in China

Design by Chloe Rawlins
Production by Anitra Alcantara
Food and prop styling by Christine Wolheim
Illustrations by Diane Tarango first appeared in a slightly different
form in *Tamales 101*

10 9 8 7 6 5 4 3 2 1

First Edition

VOLUME

U.S.	IMPERIAL	METRIC
1 tablespoon	$1/2$ fl oz	15 ml
2 tablespoons	1 fl oz	30 ml
$1/4$ cup	2 fl oz	60 ml
$1/3$ cup	3 fl oz	90 ml
$1/2$ cup	4 fl oz	120 ml
$2/3$ cup	5 fl oz ($1/4$ pint)	150 ml
$3/4$ cup	6 fl oz	180 ml
1 cup	8 fl oz ($1/3$ pint)	240 ml
$1^1/4$ cups	10 fl oz ($1/2$ pint)	300 ml
2 cups (1 pint)	16 fl oz ($2/3$ pint)	480 ml
$2^1/2$ cups	20 fl oz (1 pint)	600 ml
1 quart	32 fl oz ($1^2/3$ pints)	1 l

TEMPERATURE

FAHRENHEIT	CELSIUS/GAS MARK
250°F	120°C/gas mark $1/2$
275°F	135°C/gas mark 1
300°F	150°C/gas mark 2
325°F	160°C/gas mark 3
350°F	180 or 175°C/gas mark 4
375°F	190°C/gas mark 5
400°F	200°C/gas mark 6
425°F	220°C/gas mark 7
450°F	230°C/gas mark 8
475°F	245°C/gas mark 9
500°F	260°C

LENGTH

INCH	METRIC
$1/4$ inch	6 mm
$1/2$ inch	1.25 cm
$3/4$ inch	2 cm
1 inch	2.5 cm
6 inches ($1/2$ foot)	15 cm
12 inches (1 foot)	30 cm

WEIGHT

U.S./IMPERIAL	METRIC
$1/2$ oz	15 g
1 oz	30 g
2 oz	60 g
$1/4$ lb	115 g
$1/3$ lb	150 g
$1/2$ lb	225 g
$3/4$ lb	350 g
1 lb	450 g